BLUEPRINT

Maths Assessment Key Stage 2

David and Wendy Clemson

Stanley Thornes (Publishers) Ltd

© Text Wendy Clemson and David Clemson 1995
© Original line illustrations ST(P) Ltd 1995

The right of Wendy Clemson and David Clemson to be identified as authors of this work has been asserted by them in accordance with the Copyright, Designs and Patents Act 1988.

All rights reserved. No part of this publication may be reproduced or transmitted in any form or by any means, electronic or mechanical, including photocopy, recording or any information storage and retrieval system, without permission in writing from the publisher or under licence from the Copyright Licensing Agency Limited. Further details of such licences (for reprographic reproduction) may be obtained from the Copyright Licensing Agency Limited of 90 Tottenham Court Road, London W1P 9HE.

Material from The National Curriculum document is Crown copyright and is reproduced with the permission of the Controller of Her Majesty's Stationery Office.

First published in 1995 by:
Stanley Thornes (Publishers) Ltd
Ellenborough House
Wellington Street
CHELTENHAM GL50 1YD

A catalogue record for this book is available from the British Library.

ISBN 0 7487 1752 8

Designed and typeset by John Youé Book Design, Honiton, Devon.
Printed and bound in Great Britain.

Contents

Introduction	iv
Methods for collecting assessment information	v
How to use this book	vi
Assessment across the mathematics curriculum	1

AT1: Using and Applying Mathematics — 2
- Level 2
  - 1 Select and talk about mathematics — 2
  - 2 Mathematical language/diagram — 2
  - 3 Respond to 'what if?' — 2
- Level 3
  - 4 Solve problems — 3
  - 5 Organize, check, explain, use diagrams — 3
  - 6 Investigate a general statement — 3
- Level 4
  - 7 Problem solving — 4
  - 8 Present information/results clearly — 4
  - 9 Pattern search – own ideas — 4
- Level 5
  - 10 Carry through a task — 5
  - 11 Use symbols etc in making diagrams — 5
  - 12 Make/test generalizations — 5

AT2: Number and Algebra — 6
- Level 2
  - 1 Add/subtract to 10; numbers to 100 — 6
  - 2 Halves and quarters — 6
  - 3 Number patterns — 6
- Level 3
  - 4 Interpreting big numbers — 7
  - 5 Decimal money/approximation — 7
  - 6 Negative numbers — 7
  - 7 Add/subtract to 20 including 0 — 7
  - 8 2, 5, 10 x tables and up to 5 x 5 — 8
  - 9 Multiplication/division problems — 8
  - 10 Remainders — 8
  - 11 Patterns and computation strategies — 8
- Level 4
  - 12 Place value — 9
  - 13 Computation — 9
  - 14 Calculator problems — 9
  - 15 Fractions and percentages — 10
  - 16 Patterns, multiples, factors, squares — 10
  - 17 Formulae/equations in words — 10
  - 18 Coordinates in the first quadrant — 10
- Level 5
  - 19 Multiply/divide by 10, 100, 1,000 — 11
  - 20 Negative numbers/decimals — 11
  - 21 Fractions and percentages — 11
  - 22 Multiply and divide — 11
  - 23 Formulae and equations — 12

AT3: Shape, Space and Measures — 13
- Level 2
  - 1 Names of 2-D, 3-D shapes — 13
  - 2 Types of movement — 13
  - 3 Right angles — 13
  - 4 Measure (NSU and SU) length/mass — 14
- Level 3
  - 5 Sorting shapes — 14
  - 6 Reflective symmetry — 14
  - 7 Measure length/capacity/mass/time — 15
- Level 4
  - 8 Construct 2-D/3-D shapes; reflection — 15
  - 9 Congruence — 15
  - 10 Rotational symmetry — 16
  - 11 Measuring — 16
  - 12 Perimeter and area — 16
  - 13 Volume — 16
- Level 5
  - 14 Accurate construction of 3-D models — 17
  - 15 Angle language — 17
  - 16 Shape properties — 17
  - 17 Imperial/metric – measures/estimation — 17

AT4: Handling Data — 19
- Level 2
  - 1 Sorting objects — 19
  - 2 Gather information/construct a table — 19
- Level 3
  - 3 Table/list — 20
  - 4 Bar chart/pictogram construction — 20
  - 5 Bar chart/pictogram interpretation — 20
- Level 4
  - 6 Interpret/construct frequency diagrams — 21
  - 7 Frequency diagrams – median/mode — 21
  - 8 'Likelihood', 'evens' and 'fair' — 21
- Level 5
  - 9 Mean and range — 22
  - 10 Construct/interpret statistical diagrams — 22
  - 11 Estimate and justify probabilities — 22
  - 12 Listing all possible outcomes — 22

Copymasters 1-128

Record Sheet 1 Class Record

Record Sheet 2 Child's Record

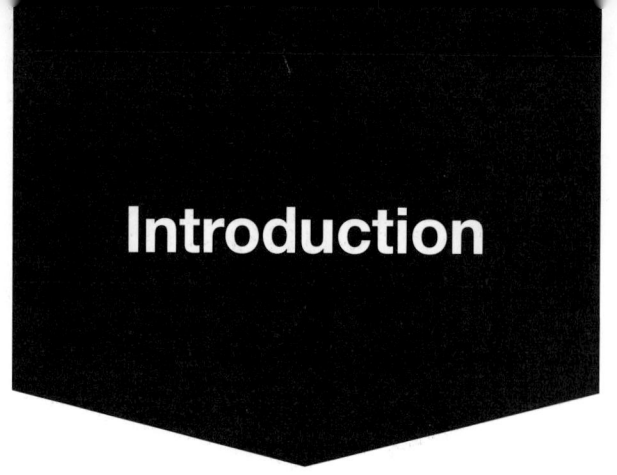

Introduction

An important part of a teacher's work is the constant assessment of children's learning. Only by assessing can we devise what children should do next and give them tasks that are appropriate. It is to support teachers in their assessment of children's work in mathematics that this book has been written. The book begins with some pointers to the methods of collecting assessment information that are available to teachers. These and the assessment tasks that follow are intended to support teachers in forming their own assessments of what children know and can do. The exercises are not intended as rigorous in-depth 'tests'. Rather they are indicators or clues to where the children have reached, and we see them as having a predominantly formative purpose.

We have deliberately made the assessment exercises as varied as possible for two reasons: firstly, so that teachers can use a variety of everyday classroom settings to glean assessment information; secondly because we believe a variety of activities is motivating for children and enables them to better demonstrate their mastery of mathematics.

BLUEPRINTS MATHS ASSESSMENT AND THE NATIONAL CURRICULUM

Blueprints Maths Assessment is a practical teacher's resource specifically tied in to the requirements of the National Curriculum for mathematics in primary schools. It offers assessment tasks which teachers can use alongside those they devise themselves, or with more formal 'tests'. *Blueprints Maths Assessment: Key Stage 1* provides tasks for children between 5 and 7 years old; *Blueprints Maths Assessment: Key Stage 2* provides tasks for children between 7 and 11 years old. Teacher's notes and assessment copymasters are combined in one book for each Key Stage. The sequence the exercises follow matches that of the content of *Mathematics in the National Curriculum (1995)*.

Blueprints Maths Assessment: Key Stage 2 provides a set of assessment tasks through Key Stage 2. The assessment exercises are arranged in four sections, each related to the assessment of work expected of children through this Key Stage: Attainment Targets 1, 2, 3 and 4, from Levels 2 to 5.

Because all four parts of the programme of study – using and applying mathematics, number and algebra, shape, space and measures, and handling data are inter-related, work in one area can be used to assess understanding in another. The settings in which we have chosen to place assessment tasks are exemplars. Teachers can use the tasks given in flexible ways. For example Task 5 in Attainment Target 4 could be used to determine a Level 4 performance in either Attainment Target 4 or Attainment Target 1.

At the start of the teacher's notes about the assessment tasks relating to each Level of each Attainment Target there is an extract from the Statutory Orders, comprising the Attainment Target title, and the appropriate Level description. Attached to each assessment task is a copymaster. In some cases the copymaster is for the teacher's use and in others for the children's use. This assessment copymaster is labelled 'A'. For all tasks there are also reassessment copymasters, labelled 'B'. Each of these appears immediately after each 'first try' copymaster. Here are some ways of using the reassessment ideas:

- for children to do as an addition to the first assessment task
- where children make mistakes on the first task, as a second try at a later date
- where a group of children are doing the task at the same time some can be given the assessment version and some the reassessment version

There are two summary record sheets at the back of the book. The first is a tick list to enable you to record which children in the class have done each task at a specific Level. The second is a tick list that can be kept for each child, showing those tasks the child has tried and which of them successfully.

RECORD KEEPING

There are photocopiable record sheets at the back of the book. Photocopy one Record Sheet 1 per class to maintain a tick list to show assessment tasks tried at a specific Level. Photocopy one Record Sheet 2 per child and tick the assessment tasks tried, those done successfully, and reassessment attempts where appropriate. This record sheet can be added to school records.

Methods for Collecting Assessment Information

There are five ways in which teachers can collect assessment information. They are as follows:

- observing
- listening
- participating
- scrutinizing written outcomes
- giving tests

To carry through assessment effectively, using any of these methods for collecting information, demands expertise that is sometimes not acknowledged. To alert you to some of the important issues to think about when choosing and using assessment methods, the following will be listed for each method:

- how to do it
- advantages
- disadvantages

OBSERVING

Teachers constantly monitor the work of a whole class and maintain an overview. While something you notice by chance can, of course, contribute to your assessments; observations need to be more deliberate in order to be systematic. You cannot expect to 'notice' all you need to see on days when you are working with the whole class. To allow you to observe, it is therefore important that there is another adult present to whom the children can turn.

Set yourself a focused brief. A general aim may not allow you to collect usable information. Take chronological notes, which will remind you of the flow of events you observed.

Make interpretations of your notes for the record as soon as you can after the session to avoid having to recall from distant memory what exactly went on.

ADVANTAGES Observations can yield a variety of information in one session. Observations can be made of a number of children working alongside one another or cooperatively. Children can be observed in the course of their 'normal' school day.

DISADVANTAGES If you have planned to observe while you monitor the whole class, your time for observation will probably be brief or sporadic. Another adult in the room would, of course, free you to observe for longer periods. The information is unpredictable, and what you hoped to observe may not happen because of the dynamic of the classroom that day.

LISTENING

Assessment information you have heard can be collected in a variety of classroom settings. You can listen to a group involved in a collaborative activity, or when they are setting up or clearing away. You can tape-record such sessions and glean assessment information by listening to the tape after school is over. You can assess by listening when you give a child individual attention. Good opportunities for assessing by listening also occur when the children are an audience to which individuals have a chance to speak.

You can help to focus the topics talked about, so that sometimes they talk about some mathematical information they have collected, how they have set down their maths work in their book, how they solved a number mystery and so on.

An additional important source of assessment information is what we hear by chance. This information is as potent as any other but needs supplementing with systematically collected information, perhaps sometimes with the help of another adult.

ADVANTAGES Listening to assess can be done, like observing, during the course of a 'normal' school day. A tape recording can augment your notes.

DISADVANTAGES There is a temptation to direct conversations and prompt children to follow your agenda and not their own (which would threaten the validity of assessments). Your own interpretations of what children have said may not always coincide with what they intended to convey, and, if you say, 'what did you mean?' or 'is this what you meant?' you may intimidate a child who wants to please you.

PARTICIPATING

When you join in with what children are doing you can not only catalyse and provoke their thinking, but also probe their thinking processes in ways that may prove impossible using other assessment collection methods. However, inevitably, when you join in an activity, the children change what they do and how they respond to the task. Thus the information you get may give more insights into how the children are working, but you have had a greater influence on what happened.

We cannot say children can do some aspect of mathematical work if they always need help, even if it is just the occasional question like, for example, 'What do you do next?' 'Where does that 3 go?' or 'I'd look at the one you have just done if I were you'. Thus we have to be circumspect about assessments made on the sole basis of information gathered while you are participating in the task.

ADVANTAGES   It may well involve you in behaving just as you do at any other time in class, and you can be yourself. It can be more rewarding to you, the assessor, than trying to maintain a distance from the children you are assessing.

DISADVANTAGES   You cannot record any notes at the time. Focusing your assessment while involved in the dynamic of conversation and action can be difficult. Assessments are probably less problematic if the teacher is not involved, so perhaps participating should not be a first-choice method for getting assessment information.

SCRUTINIZING WRITTEN OUTCOMES
By this we do not mean marking, though it may be part of the process of assessment. The idea of a written examination as a way of demonstrating achievement probably affects how everyone, including children, parents and teachers, feel about what they put on paper. It is regarded as the primary source of learning evidence. It can indeed give indicators about recording skills and understanding of a necessary sequence of steps in mathematical operations. For much of the learning that children do in the junior school, however, the other ways of collecting assessment information are more potent in determining children's *understanding* of mathematics.

ADVANTAGES   You can actually do the assessing with a child while they sit alongside you in class. It can be very important in letting children know about the standards you apply. It can also help to show children how they themselves can determine what their best is. You can also assess children's work outside the school day. The assessment information is complete and concrete, and available for review. This whole record of information and interpretations can be stored as a part of the child's progress record or portfolio.

DISADVANTAGES   What is written down tells you little about whether the child understands what they have done. There can be aspects of written work which threaten to contaminate our judgements. For example, we may judge neatly presented work as better than less-tidy work, whether or not it matches the standard of less-tidy work in terms of content.

GIVING TESTS
This is an important method of collecting assessment information throughout the education system. However, it has little place in this book, for we do not view the tasks we have devised as being tests in the strictest sense. They are intended rather as indicators to support teachers' own judgements. Teachers may, however, wish to support their assessments by selecting a few tasks and assembling them into a 'home-made' test across Attainment Targets or Levels for individuals or groups of children. The advantages and disadvantages of giving tests are legion, and beyond the scope of this book.

FURTHER READING
Clemson, D and W Clemson, *The Really Practical Guide to Primary Assessment*, Stanley Thornes, 1991
Clemson, D and W Clemson, *Mathematics in the Early Years,* Routledge, 1994
Duncan, A and W Dunn, *What Primary Teachers Should Know about Assessment*, Hodder and Stoughton, 1988
The Mathematical Association, *Maths Talk*, Stanley Thornes, 1987
Mitchell, C and V Koshy, *Effective Teacher Assessment*, Hodder and Stoughton, 1993

How to use this book

This book has been tied to National Curriculum Attainment Targets so that the assessment tasks can be accessed easily. Within each of the sections – using and applying mathematics, number and algebra, and shape, space and measures – the tasks have been arranged by Level, with Level 2 exercises first, and so on. Our intention has been to provide a bank of short assessment tasks covering all Attainment Targets. However, we hope that readers will, rather than taking the book wholesale, choose and use those tasks which they find most useful, to support their own assessment judgements.

The copymasters (labelled 'A') are also marked to indicate to which AT and Level they refer. Reassessment copymasters are labelled 'B'. At the end of the book are two record sheets, enabling you to keep a class record and a record of the assessment tasks tried by each child.

Assessment across the Mathematics Curriculum

Children's learning in particular areas of mathematics should contribute to their understanding in others. Work can sometimes provide assessments for more than one Attainment Target. Here are examples showing mathematical settings for assessment in AT1 where assessments in AT2, AT3 or AT4 could also be made.

AT1, LEVEL 2

In order to give children independence of action in carrying through maths tasks, try letting them gather their own resources from the bank of resources in the classroom. They could then, for example:

- show that they choose a 30 cm ruler to measure a book, but a 1-metre stick to measure the classroom (also AT3)
- collect a variety of small things of different shapes and materials for sorting (also AT2 and AT4)

Mathematical language both oral and written can be shown, when, for example, they:

- arrange models for a mathematical display (also AT3)
- make a little book on how much of which foods are consumed by a variety of pets and read aloud from it (also AT2 and AT4)

During discussion times you can offer children opportunities to make predictions like the following:

- four people went home to dinner last Friday and three on the Friday before that. It is Friday again today; how many do you think will go home today? What will be the likely total number of people going home for dinner for all three Fridays? (also AT2)
- what usually happens after play? (also AT2)
- what might happen if we put more cubes on this side of the balance? (also AT3)

AT1, LEVEL 3

To let children demonstrate that they can solve problems they can be given open-ended maths activities. Here are some examples from *Blueprints Maths Investigations*:

- design a badge or logo using symmetry (Investigation 40; also AT3)
- invent a shape trail (Investigation 42; also AT3)
- explore the Möbius strip (Investigation 27; also AT3)

You can see from their efforts how they organize what they are doing and whether they checked their work.

Children can discuss their thinking and their mathematics when reporting to the class about their work:

- how they solved a number problem involving pocket-money toys in the classroom shop (also AT2)
- how they recorded what they found out about the life cycle of a frog, moth or dragonfly (also AT3 and AT4)

Look at a variety of ways of presenting findings, using symbols and diagrams, and let the children choose and adapt that which they think appropriate in a variety of situations. For example:

- survey data (also AT2 and AT4)
- designing a contents plan for a maths resource cupboard (also AT2 and AT4)

While investigating general statements like the following, children enhance their competence in number work:

- all even numbers are divisible by 2 (also AT2)
- the product of any number multiplied by 9 will reduce to the digit 9 (also AT2)

AT1, LEVEL 4

Children can be developing and demonstrating their own strategies for solving problems while, for example, working up mental computation skills, using two-digit and three-digit numbers (also AT2).

Their organizing ability regarding information and results is evident in the way they record, for example, temperature change throughout the day and in how they construct a line graph (also AT2).

They are trying out pattern ideas when they look at prime numbers, square roots and the like (also AT2).

AT1, LEVEL 5

The children are now able to carry through mathematical research tasks, like these:

- studies of classmates' preferences regarding music, food and holidays
- attitudes to uniform, school hours, bedtimes, paper rounds, jewellery

Such research may involve work in AT2, AT3 and AT4.

They use symbols and diagrams, for example pie charts (also AT4).

The children are offered opportunities to make general statements by being given investigations like the following which come from *Blueprints Maths Investigations*:

- angles in 2-D shapes (Investigation 73; also AT2)
- faces, vertices and edges of shapes (Investigation 74; also AT3)
- snooker ball puzzles (Investigation 80; also AT3)

Similarly, the assessment tasks in this book can be used flexibly. How a child tackles a task can provide assessment information in more than one area of mathematics.

AT1: Using and Applying Mathematics

LEVEL 2

Level Description

Pupils select the mathematics for some classroom activities. They discuss their work using familiar mathematical language and are beginning to represent it using symbols and simple diagrams. They ask and respond appropriately to questions including 'What would happen if...?'.

TASK 1 — SELECT AND TALK ABOUT MATHEMATICS A/B
C1-2

Resources
None.

Organization
This task should be done individually with the teacher.

What you do
Ask the child to explain how they would go about finding out the answers to the each of the problems depicted on copymaster C1. Listen for their choice of mathematical operation and measuring tools, and mathematical vocabulary.

What the child does
The child talks to the teacher about how they would tackle the problems on the copymaster, explaining the mathematics and tools they might use.

Key question
Can the child choose appropriate mathematical strategies?

Reassessment
Let the child talk to you about the problem situations on copymaster C2 (select and talk about mathematics B).

TASK 2 — MATHEMATICAL LANGUAGE/DIAGRAM A/B
C3-4

Resources
Games involving mathematical elements eg dominoes, snakes and ladders, beetle drive, bingo, squared paper.

Organization
The child needs to work alone on this task, the first part in a one-to-one with the teacher.

What you do
Give the child a game and allow them a little time to familiarize themselves with it. Then ask them to explain to you how it is set up, played and won. Note down on copymaster C3 whether the child is able to do so using mathematical ideas, and the mathematical vocabulary and concepts the child uses.

If the child has invented a new way of playing the game this is fine, for it is a vehicle for mathematical ideas. For example, they may talk about the possible numbers to show on the die, or how many moves can be made. Then read aloud the jelly bean data found on the copymaster and give the child the data strip which can be cut from the bottom of the copymaster. Give the child squared paper if they need it.

What the child does
The child talks to the teacher about how to play a game, using mathematical ideas. They are then asked to complete a mathematical diagram using information given to them by the teacher.

Key question
Can the child use mathematical language and create a simple mathematical diagram?

Reassessment
Using copymaster C4 (mathematical language/diagram B) ask the child to describe the playing of another game and create a mathematical diagram using the pocket toys data.

TASK 3 — RESPOND TO 'WHAT IF?' A/B
C5-6

Resources
None.

Organization
This is done individually with the teacher's help.

What you do
Describe each situation on C5 while the child looks on.

What the child does
The child explains what they think would be the result of each event or action, using mathematical ideas and vocabulary. For example, in the first one we might expect the child to say that three people are probably heavier than two, and that this side of the see-saw would go down.

Key question
Can the child make mathematical predictions?

Reassessment
Use copymaster C6 (respond to 'What if?' B) and proceed as for assessment.

LEVEL 3

Level Description

Pupils try different approaches and find ways of overcoming difficulties that arise when they are solving problems. They are beginning to organise their work and check results. Pupils discuss their mathematical work and are beginning to explain their thinking. They use and interpret mathematical symbols and diagrams. Pupils show that they understand a general statement by finding particular examples that match it.

TASK 4 — SOLVE PROBLEMS A/B
C7-8

TASK 5 — ORGANIZE, CHECK, EXPLAIN, USE DIAGRAMS A/B
C9-10

Resources
Ten classmates to give information, and rough paper, squared paper.

Organization
Children could work in pairs at the information-getting stage. The presentation of written work needs to be done alone, and any feedback to the teacher or class should be done individually.

What you do
Give the child the copymaster C7 and ask them to find out from ten classmates their first and second career choices from the copymaster list. They can add their own choices and then order and present the information. Allow the child to discuss the problems they had, with you or before a group of children who are not involved in doing the assessment task.

What the child does
The child has to collect the appropriate information from a group of classmates, overcome any difficulties, organize the outcomes and report back about how the problems were solved. Information getting can be done in pairs.

Key question
Can the child adopt a variety of strategies when problem solving?

Reassessment
Give the child copymaster C8 (solve problems B) and ask them to use a similar sample as for the assessment. Resources include postcard copies of famous masters or colour photocopies from a good quality art book. They show around the pictures of the work of six artists and the children name their two favourite artists based on the what they see. The child should organize the information and report back on how any problems were solved.

Resources
A permission note to send to parents for the children may need to make some notes at home, and rough paper; the *Radio* or *TV Times* might also be helpful.

Organization
This needs to be done by each child individually.

What you do
Give each child copymaster C9 and some rough paper. Ask them to complete the information-getting task in rough, and then make a fair copy on a mathematical diagram.

What the child does
Each child keeps a note of their TV viewing for a week. They can keep a continuous record at home, or compile a list of their viewing first thing the next morning when they arrive at school. Friday's viewing should be written up at the weekend. They then need to organize their results in a diagram and show and explain it.

Key question
Can the child organize, check and explain results and construct a mathematical diagram?

Reassessment
Give the child C10 (organize, check, explain, use diagrams B) and ask them to make rough records and construct a diagram which they can show and explain.

TASK 6 — INVESTIGATE A GENERAL STATEMENT A/B
C11-12

Resources
Set of dominoes, rough paper, calculator.

Organization
This is an individual task.

What you do
Explain to the child that to do the task they have to test out the general statement by looking at specific examples and asking whether the general statement holds. You will be able to check in discussion or from the child's rough notes that they have tried out specific examples, ordered their findings and are confident of their conclusions.

What the child does
The child has to explore the set of dominoes to check whether the general statement holds, making rough notes on the copymaster, and explaining their conclusions.

Key question
Can the child investigate and verify general statements?

Reassessment
Give the child C12 (investigate general statement B) and a calculator and allow them to work through the task, explaining to you their conclusion and how they arrived at it.

LEVEL 4

Level Description

Pupils are developing their own strategies for solving problems and are using these strategies both in working within mathematics and in applying mathematics to practical contexts. They present information and results in a clear and organised way, explaining the reasons for their presentation. They search for a pattern by trying out ideas of their own.

TASK 7 — PROBLEM SOLVING A/B

C13-14

Resources
None essential, but children may wish to use information about how paint is supplied.

Organization
The child needs to work individually.

What you do
Give the child copymaster C13 and establish that they understand the task in hand.

What the child does
The child records answers to aspects of the problem set out on copymaster C13.

Key question
Can the child devise their own strategies to solve problems?

Reassessment
Give the child copymaster C14 (problem solving B) and allow them to work up answers to aspects of the problem.

TASK 8 — PRESENT INFORMATION/RESULTS CLEARLY A/B

C15-16

Resources
Food packaging showing ingredients, squared paper.

Organization
This is an individual task, but children may like to explain their results to a class or group. (This would have to be done after everyone has completed the task.)

What you do
Give the child access to food packaging and copymaster C15.

What the child does
The child inspects the food packaging, makes rough notes and then draws up a chart of results which they can explain.

Key question
Can the child present information and results clearly?

Reassessment
Give the child copymaster C16 (present information/results clearly B) on which they record rough notes.

TASK 9 — PATTERN SEARCH – OWN IDEAS A/B

C17-18

Resources
Calculators.

Organization
This is an individual task.

What you do
Give the child copymaster C17 and access to a calculator.

What the child does
The child works on the copymaster, using a calculator if necessary.

Key question
Can the child put their own ideas to use in searching for a pattern?

Reassessment
Give the child copymaster C18 (pattern search – own ideas B) and a calculator.

LEVEL 5

Level Description
In order to carry through tasks and solve mathematical problems, pupils identify and obtain necessary information; they check their results, considering whether these are sensible. Pupils show understanding of situations by describing them mathematically, using symbols, words and diagrams. They make general statements of their own, based on evidence they have produced, and give an explanation of their reasoning.

TASK 10 — CARRY THROUGH A TASK A/B
C19-20

Resources
It should be part of the task that the children search for their own resources, but have available to them paper to work on and information related to symmetry. This may include Lewis Carroll's *Through the Looking Glass*, books of art and design, mathematical dictionaries and text books, examples of illuminated lettering and letters in different styles and fonts, information about handedness.

Organization
Some of this work can be done in pairs or by groups of children, but the teacher will need to be vigilant about the extent to which each child has contributed to the task in hand.

What you do
Talk through the task with the children and make sure they are well resourced. Observe their activities and, by judicious questioning, establish that they are all making sustained and appropriate contributions.

What the child does
Working alone, or in a group, the child has to analyse and comment on the concepts and information contained in a newspaper article.

Key question
Can the child carry through a mathematical problem solving task?

Reassessment
Give the child copymaster C20 (carry through a task B) and a range of educational supplements from some national newspapers.

TASK 11 — USE SYMBOLS ETC IN MAKING DIAGRAMS A/B

C21-22

Resources
Access to the school library when there are going to be children using it, card, coloured pens and scissors, rough paper, and squared paper.

Organization
The diagrams have to be made by each child individually. It would be ideal if the information-getting task was done alone too, but this may be impractical.

What you do
Give the child copymaster C22 and access to the required resources. If the children are working in groups on the information-getting task, the teacher needs to be certain that all children collecting information are competent at doing this.

What the child does
The child follows the directions on the copymaster in order to gather data which they can present on mathematical diagrams.

Key question
Can the child explain their understanding by creating a mathematical diagram?

Reassessment
Give the child copymaster C22 (use symbols etc in making diagrams B) and invite them to collect the data and create mathematical diagrams. Resources required are access to class teachers and dice.

TASK 12 — MAKE/TEST GENERALIZATIONS A/B

C23-24

Resources
Access to classmates for information, tapes and measures.

Organization
The record of what they have done must be made individually by each child. Information may have to be gathered in pairs or by groups. The child has to explain what they have done, either to you or to a group of classmates.

What you do
Let the child find out the information, carry through the task and make charts showing the outcomes, which they can explain.

What the child does
The child finds out the information, carries through the task and makes charts showing the outcomes, which they can explain.

Key question
Can the child make general statements and put them to the test?

Reassessment
Give the child copymaster C24 and invite them to carry through the task.

AT2: Number and Algebra

LEVEL 2

Level Description

Pupils count sets of objects reliably, and use mental recall of addition and subtraction facts to 10. They have begun to understand the place value of each digit in a number and use this to order numbers up to 100. They choose the appropriate operation when solving addition and subtraction problems. They identify and use halves and quarters, such as half of a rectangle or a quarter of eight objects. They recognise sequences of numbers, including odd and even numbers.

TASK 1 — ADD/SUBTRACT TO 10; NUMBERS TO 100 A/B

Resources
None.

Organization
This is an individual task to be done in a 'test' situation.

What you do
Give the child copymaster C25 to complete.

What the child does
The child fills in the answers on copymaster C25.

Key question
Can the child add and subtract to ten and understand place value?

Reassessment
Give the child copymaster C26 (add/subtract to 10 and numbers to 100 B) to complete.

TASK 2 — HALVES AND QUARTERS A/B

Resources
Coloured pencils.

Organization
This is an individual task.

What you do
Give the child copymaster C27 to complete.

What the child does
The child completes the puzzles on copymaster C27.

Key question
Does the child understand the concepts of a half and a quarter?

Reassessment
Give the child copymaster C28 to complete.

TASK 3 — NUMBER PATTERNS A/B

Resources
None.

Organization
This is an individual task.

What you do
Give the child copymaster C29 to complete.

What the child does
The child completes the patterns on copymaster C29.

Key question
Can the child identify and continue number patterns?

Reassessment
Give the child copymaster C30 to complete, along with red or blue pens or coloured pencils.

LEVEL 3

Level Description

Pupils show understanding of place value in numbers up to 1000 and use this to make approximations. They have begun to use decimal notation and to recognise negative numbers, in contexts such as money, temperature and calculator displays. Pupils use mental recall of addition and subtraction facts to 20 in solving problems involving larger numbers. They use mental recall of the 2, 5 and 10 multiplication tables, and others up to 5 x 5, in solving whole number problems involving multiplication or division, including those that give rise to remainders. Pupils use calculator methods where numbers include several digits. They have begun to develop mental strategies, and use them to find methods for adding and subtracting numbers with at least two digits.

TASK 4 — INTERPRETING BIG NUMBERS A/B
C31-32

Resources
None.

Organization
This task should be done individually in a 'test' situation.

What you do
Give the child copymaster C31 to complete.

What the child does
The child has to inspect the numbers on the copymaster to determine how many hundreds, tens or units in them, and then create some appropriate numbers.

Key question
Can the child interpret big numbers?

Reassessment
Give the child copymaster C32 to complete.

TASK 5 — DECIMAL MONEY/APPROXIMATION A/B

C33-34

Resources
Calculators for checking work, if you think them appropriate.

Organization
This is an individual task.

What you do
Give the child copymaster C33 to complete. Work out the answers ready for marking.

What the child does
The child has to work out the totals and change in the calculations on the copymaster, and make some approximations.

Key question
Is the child confident in the use of decimal money and can the child approximate?

Reassessment
Give the child copymaster C34 to complete.

TASK 6 — NEGATIVE NUMBERS A/B

C35-36

Resources
None.

Organization
This is an individual task.

What you do
Give the child copymaster C35 to complete.

What the child does
Though the Level description ties negative numbers into a context, this task has been set just to determine whether children know what negative numbers look like.

Key question
Can the child recognize and assign negative numbers?

Reassessment
Give the child C36 (negative numbers B) to complete.

TASK 7 — ADD/SUBTRACT TO 20 INCLUDING 0 A/B

C37-38

Resources
None.

Organization
This should be done individually in a 'test' situation.

What you do
Give the child copymaster C37 to complete.

What the child does
The child has to fill in the missing numbers on the copymaster.

A thorough knowledge of number bonds up to 20 is the starting point for problem solving with larger numbers. To demonstrate competence, the child should do this quickly and accurately.

Key question
Can the child add and subtract whole numbers up to 20 with ease and confidence?

Reassessment
Give the child copymaster C38 (add/subtract to 20, including zero) to complete.

TASK 8 — 2, 5, 10 X TABLES AND UP TO 5 X 5 A/B (C39-40)

Resources
None.

Organization
This is an individual task.

What you do
Give the child copymaster C39 to complete.

What the child does
The child has to write out the two, five and ten times tables and answer some puzzles.

A knowledge of the tables in sequence is, of course, not as important as the ability to recall multiplication facts in isolation. Nonetheless, knowledge of the pattern of products in sequence can be a useful aid to the memory.

Key question
Does the child know his two, five and ten times tables and all products up to five times five?

Reassessment
Give the child copymaster C40 (2, 5 and 10 x tables and up to 5 x 5 B) to complete.

TASK 9 — MULTIPLICATION/DIVISION PROBLEMS A/B (C41-42)

Resources
Rough paper.

Organization
This should be done individually.

What you do
Give the child paper for rough notes and copymaster C41.

What the child does
The child has to solve the problems on the copymaster.

Key question
Can the child solve problems involving multiplication and division?

Reassessment
Give the child copymaster C42 (multiplication/division problems B) to work on.

TASK 10 — REMAINDERS A/B (C43-44)

Resources
None.

Organization
This task is to be done individually.

What you do
Give the child copymaster C43 to complete.

What the child does
The child has to put in the remainders; then answers, including remainders, to some calculations.

Key question
Can the child demonstrate an understanding of remainders?

Reassessment
Give the child copymaster C44 (remainders B) to complete.

TASK 11 — PATTERNS AND COMPUTATION STRATEGIES A/B (C45-46)

Resources
Counting aids if required, calculators for follow up work.

Organization
This task must be done alone by each child.

What you do
Give the child copymaster C45. Make sure they understand that in the second part of this task they have to write down the steps they take in working out the calculations. After they have finished the tasks ask about the patterns and strategies in use. You can also supplement this task with some calculator computations.

What the child does
The child has to continue the patterns and show their computation strategies on copymaster C45. When they have completed these they should talk to the teacher about what they have done.

Key question
Can the child recognize and use number patterns?

Reassessment
Give the child copymaster C46 (patterns and computation strategies B) and proceed as above.

LEVEL 4

Level Description

Pupils use their understanding of place value to multiply and divide whole numbers by 10 or 100. In solving number problems, pupils use a range of mental and written methods of computation with the four operations, including mental recall of multiplication facts up to 10 x 10. They add and subtract decimals to two places. In solving problems with or without a calculator, pupils check the reasonableness of their results by reference to their knowledge of the context or to the size of the numbers. They recognise approximate proportions of a whole and use simple fractions and percentages to describe these. Pupils explore and describe number patterns, and relationships including multiple, factor and square. They have begun to use simple formulae expressed in words. Pupils use and interpret co-ordinates in the first quadrant.

TASK 12 — PLACE VALUE A/B
C47-48

Resources
None.

Organization
This should be done individually.

What you do
Ask the child to carefully fill in the answers on copymaster C47. Remind the child that multiplication or division is required before they make an entry in the answer box.

What the child does
The child should do the multiplications and divisions on the copymaster and make entries in the answer boxes.

Key question
Does the child understand place value?

Reassessment
Give the child C48 (place value B) to work on.

TASK 13 — COMPUTATION A/B
C49-50

Resources
None as this is to be done without counting aids.

Organization
The calculations set down on the copymaster are to be done by each child without collaboration. The purpose is to test methods used, so while answers are important, the way the child does the task is of paramount importance.

What you do
Compile fifteen mental arithmetic questions. Give the children C49 and observe them while they work to ascertain the methods in use or talk to each child when they have done the task to find out how they worked. Then give the children a mental arithmetic test in a group setting.

What the child does
The child works through the computations and completes a mental arithmetic test, entering the answers on the copymaster.

Key question
Is the child using a variety of methods in computation?

Reassessment
Give the child C50 to complete. Work out a mental arithmetic test. Proceed as for assessment A.

TASK 14 — CALCULATOR PROBLEMS A/B
C51-52

Resources
Calculators, rough paper, access to the hall and a school chair; measuring tapes, the number of children in the school aged 9, 10 and 11; from the school cook, the 'weight' of a chip portion and the likely number of portions eaten each day.

Organization
The information-getting stage can be done in pairs. Each child must do the calculations on a calculator on their own.

What you do
Give the children access to the resources required and the appropriate time for collection of data. Ask the children to check that the answers are reasonable.

What the child does
The child collects information, uses a calculator to solve problems, and looks carefully at the answers to make sure they are reasonable.

Key question
Can the child solve problems, checking that the answers are reasonable?

Reassessment
Give the children C52. Resources required are details of the school day and school year. Proceed as for assessment A.

TASK 15 — FRACTIONS AND PERCENTAGES A/B (C53-54)

Resources
None.

Organization
This is an individual task in a 'test' situation.

What you do
Give the child copymaster C53 to work on.

What the child does
The child fills in the fractions and percentages.

Key question
Does the child understand simple fractions and percentages?

Reassessment
Let the child complete copymaster C54 (fractions and percentages B).

TASK 16 — PATTERNS, MULTIPLES, FACTORS, SQUARES A/B (C55-56)

Resources
None.

Organization
This is an individual task.

What you do
Give the child copymaster C55 to complete. Note that the number 'trees' are examples and not the only ones that produce the numbers shown.

What the child does
The child has to work out the answers to the puzzles on the copymaster.

Key question
Does the child recognize primes, factors and squares?

Reassessment
Give the child copymaster C56 to complete.

TASK 17 — FORMULAE/EQUATIONS IN WORDS A/B (C57-58)

Resources
Rough paper.

Organization
This is an individual task.

What you do
Give the children copymaster C57 to complete. Ensure that they understand that they are to determine the general statement in each case.

What the child does
The child has to determine what the general equation or formula is in each case.

Key question
Is the child able to use formulae expressed in words?

Reassessment
Give the child copymaster C58 to complete.

TASK 18 — COORDINATES IN THE FIRST QUADRANT A/B (C59-60)

Resources
Ruler and red pencil.

Organization
This should be done in a 'test' situation.

What you do
Give the child copymaster C59 and make sure they realize they have to draw in and mark up the axes before they start.

What the child does
The child has to draw two shapes on the squared paper.

Key question
Can the child use and interpret coordinates in the first quadrant?

Reassessment
Give the child copymaster C60 to work on.

LEVEL 5

Level Description

Pupils use their understanding of place value to multiply and divide whole numbers and decimals by 10, 100 and 1000. They order, add and subtract negative numbers in context. They use all four operations with decimals to two places. They calculate fractional or percentage parts of quantities and measurements, using a calculator where appropriate. Pupils understand and use an appropriate non-calculator method for solving problems that involve multiplying and dividing any three-digit by any two-digit number. They check their solutions by applying inverse operations or estimating using approximations. They construct, express in symbolic form, and use simple formulae involving one or two operations.

TASK 19 — MULTIPLY/DIVIDE BY 10, 100, 1,000 A/B
C61-62

Resources
None.

Organization
This is a quick task for children to do individually.

What you do
Give the children C61. This could be done, for example, by a whole class, at the beginning or end of a session.

What the child does
The child has to enter answers on the copymaster.

Key question
Does the child understand place value?

Reassessment
Let the child work on copymaster C62.

TASK 20 — NEGATIVE NUMBERS/DECIMALS A/B

C63-64

Resources
None.

Organization
This should be done individually.

What you do
Ask the child to work out and fill in the answers on copymaster C63.

What the child does
The child has to complete the calculations.

Key question
Can the child add and subtract negative numbers and work on all four operations with decimals?

Reassessment
Ask the child to complete the calculations on C64.

TASK 21 — FRACTIONS AND PERCENTAGES A/B
C65-66

Resources
Calculators, rough paper.

Organization
This task needs to be done individually.

What you do
Provide the child with copymaster C65 and a calculator.

What the child does
The child completes the fraction and percentage puzzles.

Key question
Can the child calculate fractions and percentages?

Reassessment
Give the child copymaster C66 to work on.

TASK 22 — MULTIPLY AND DIVIDE A/B
C67-68

Resources
Rough paper.

Organization
While this is an individual task, after they have done it, children could discuss their methods with the teacher in a group.

What you do
In working through the problems on copymaster C67, permit the child access to rough paper only. Ask the children to discuss how they checked that their answers were correct.

What the child does
The children have to use their own methods to solve problems involving multiplication and division of two-digit and three-digit numbers. If you want to see that they have checked their answers they should discuss their checking strategies with you.

Key question
Can the child multiply and divide two-digit and three-digit numbers and check that the answers are reasonable?

Reassessment
Give the child C68 and proceed as for assessment A.

TASK 23 — FORMULAE AND EQUATIONS A/B
C69-70

Resources
None.

Organization
This is an individual task.

What you do
Enable the child to work through the tasks on C69.

What the child does
The child has to fill in the tables on copymaster C69.

Key question
Can the child use simple formulae?

Reassessment
Let the child work on copymaster C70.

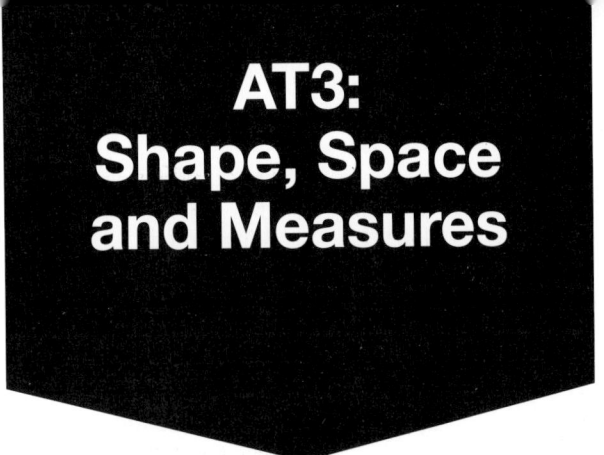

AT3: Shape, Space and Measures

> **LEVEL 2**
>
> **Level Description**
>
> Pupils use mathematical names for common 3-D and 2-D shapes and describe their properties, including numbers of sides and corners. They distinguish between straight and turning movements, understand angle as a measurement of turn, and recognise right angles in turns. They have begun to use everyday non-standard and standard units to measure length and mass.

TASK 1 — NAMES OF 2-D, 3-D SHAPES A/B

C71-72

Resources
Coloured pencils if you wish.

Organization
This is an individual task.

What you do
Give the child copymaster C71 and ask them to join each shape to its name. They can use a different colour for each if you wish. They should then record how many sides or faces and vertices each has.

What the child does
The child has to join each shape to its name, and then write in numerals to show the number of sides or faces and corners. This is a quick task and so this sheet may be combined with others to make a little 'multi-page test'.

Key question
Can the child name shapes and describe them?

Reassessment
Give the child C72 and proceed as for assessment.

TASK 2 — TYPES OF MOVEMENT A/B

C73-74

Resources
Access to the hall for a series of dance sessions

Organization
This assessment task involves a series of dance lessons. It is therefore best done in a group or whole class setting.

What you do
Conduct a series of three dance sessions which include the kinds of moves indicated on copymaster C73. Record the children's achievements on the copymaster as soon as possible after the lessons.

What the child does
The child is required to follow instructions during a series of dance sessions in order to demonstrate that they know straight and turning movements and understand angle as a measure of turn.

Key question
Can the child demonstrate that they know about straight and turning movements and that angle is a measure of turn?

Reassessment
Conduct another series of dance lessons entitled Space Experience using copymaster C74 (types of movement B) as a recording sheet. This will enable the children to demonstrate their understanding of types of movement.

TASK 3 — RIGHT ANGLES A/B

C75-76

Resources
None.

Organization
This is an individual task.

What you do
Give the child copymaster C75 to use. This should be a quick job, so this sheet could be used with others to make a 'test'.

What the child does
The child has to find and mark right angles on C75.

Key question
Can the child recognize right angles?

Reassessment
Give the child copymaster C76 (right angles B) to work on.

TASK 4 — MEASURE (NSU AND SU) LENGTH/MASS A/B
C77-78

Resources
Access to things to measure and rough paper.

Organization
Children need to work around the classroom and school for this task. It can be done in pairs or groups, so long as every child gets a chance to make decisions and measurements. The writing up can be done individually.

What you do
Assign the children to groups. Make sure they understand that they should all get a chance to make measurements. Observe the children while they are at work. Invite them to make a good copy of their work on copymaster C77.

What the child does
The child has to work with or alongside others in making a variety of measurements. They then write these up and complete the further challenge on the copymaster.

Key question
Can the child measure length and mass?

Reassessment
Give the children copymaster C78 and let them do some measuring, writing up the copymaster as their best copy.

LEVEL 3 — Level Description
Pupils classify 3-D and 2-D shapes in various ways using mathematical properties such as reflective symmetry. They use non-standard units and standard metric units of length, capacity, mass and time, in a range of contexts.

TASK 5 — SORTING SHAPES A/B
C79-80

Resources
Bought-in geometric shapes, both 2-D and 3-D.

Organization
This can be done as a group with teacher participation.

What you do
In short sessions, maybe of ten minutes each over a few days, lay out before the children the 2-D shapes. Allow each child turns at 'sorting out' and listen to their explanations for how they have done each sort. Over a number of sessions, establish whether the child is competent, and complete the copymaster. Carry through some sorts for 3-D shapes in the same way. Also, during both 2-D and 3-D sessions do some sorts yourself and allow the children to puzzle out the criteria you have used. Also allow each child to do some sorts for the others in the group to inspect. Record notes on the child's performance on copymaster C79.

What the child does
The child sorts shapes according to given criteria and identify the criteria used by the teacher and other children in sorts.

Key question
Can the child group shapes according to mathematical criteria?

Reassessment
Using card 2-D shapes and 'junk model packaging' allow the child to do some sorting and identify the criteria used in sorts done by the teacher and other children. Use copymaster C80 (sorting shapes B) to record their performance.

TASK 6 — REFLECTIVE SYMMETRY A/B
C81-82

Resources
Coloured pencils.

Organization
This task must be done individually.

What you do
Give the child copymaster C81 and ask them to think carefully before putting a coloured ring around pictures showing symmetry.

What the child does
The child has to ring those pictures on copymaster C81 that show reflective symmetry.

Key question
Can the child recognize reflective symmetry in pictures?

Reassessment
Give the child copymaster C82 (reflective symmetry B) and proceed as for assessment A.

TASK 7 — MEASURE LENGTH/CAPACITY/MASS/TIME A/B
(C83-84)

Resources
Access to a wide variety of things to measure in the classroom and the school, metric tapes and measuring sticks, a balance and metric 'weights', minute and second timers.

Organization
This work can take much time and it may speed the measuring stage if children work in pairs or in threes.

What you do
Give the child copymaster C83 and access to things to measure and measuring tools. Assign children to appropriate work groups for this task.

What the child does
The child has to measure a variety of things in and around the classroom, using non-standard and metric units.

Key question
Can the child measure length, capacity, mass and time?

Reassessment
Give the child copymaster C84 (measuring length, capacity, mass and time B) to work on.

Level Description
Pupils make 3-D mathematical models by linking given faces or edges, draw common 2-D shapes in different orientations on grids, and identify congruent shapes and orders of rotational symmetry. They reflect simple shapes in a mirror line. They choose and use appropriate units and instruments, interpreting, with appropriate accuracy, numbers on a range of measuring instruments. They find perimeters of simple shapes, find areas by counting squares, and find volumes by counting cubes.

TASK 8 — CONSTRUCT 2-D/3-D SHAPES; REFLECTION A/B
(C85-86)

Resources
Rulers, set squares, protractors, compasses, squared paper.

Organization
There are a number of things for the child to do in this task, and it may be appropriate to allow them to do it over a period of perhaps several weeks or half a term. Each drawing does need to be done by the child alone, but they may have the chance to do some of these in the course of work in other parts of the curriculum.

What you do
Either record on the copymaster when the child has done each construction listed in the course of their normal school work, or set a range of drawing tasks for the child to work through, matching those on the copymaster. Record remarks at the bottom of the copymaster.

What the child does
The child has to draw accurately a number of shapes, nets for shapes, and reflect shapes in a mirror line.

Key question
Can the child draw shapes and nets accurately, and reflect shapes in a mirror line?

Reassessment
Give the child copymaster C86 (construct 2-D/3-D shapes and reflection B) as a personal record on which to record when they have successfully done the parts of the task. They can then file it in their portfolio or it can be added to the records.

TASK 9 — CONGRUENCE A/B
(C87-88)

Resources
None.

Organization
This task should be done individually.

What you do
Give the child copymaster C87 to complete.

What the child does
The child has to label the congruent shapes on the copymaster.

Key question
Does the child understand what congruence means?

Reassessment
Give the child C88 (congruence B) to complete.

TASK 10 — ROTATIONAL SYMMETRY A/B

C89-90

Resources
Coloured pencils or crayons.

Organization
This is an individual task.

What you do
Ask the child to complete the task on the copymaster.

What the child does
The child has to complete symmetrical pictures and identify and colour some.

Key question
Can the child recognize rotational symmetry?

Reassessment
Give the child copymaster C90 (rotational symmetry B) and proceed as for assessment A.

TASK 11 — MEASURING A/B

C91-92

Resources
A variety of measuring tools from which the children can choose, including, for example, measuring tapes, balances and 'weights', measuring jugs, timers; access to things to measure.

Organization
Ideally this should be done as an individual task (except for finding the circumference of a friend's forearm) but this may be impracticable. If the children work in twos, it is important that the teacher observes the taking of measurements to check that it is being done carefully and as accurately as possible with the instruments available.

What you do
Observe the children as they take a series of measurements.

What the child does
The child has to choose appropriate instruments and take a variety of measurements.

Key question
Can the child choose and use appropriate measuring instruments?

Reassessment
Give the child C92 and proceed as for the assessment.

TASK 12 — PERIMETER AND AREA A/B

C93-94

Resources
None.

Organization
This is an individual task.

What you do
Give the child copymaster C93 to complete.

What the child does
The child finds the perimeters and areas listed on the copymaster.

Key question
Can the child find perimeters and areas?

Reassessment
Give the child copymaster C94 (perimeter and area B) to complete.

TASK 13 — VOLUME A/B

C95-96

Resources
None.

Organization
This task should be done individually.

What you do
Give the child copymaster C95 to complete.

What the child does
The child has to determine the volumes of the shapes on the copymaster.

Key question
Can the child determine volumes?

Reassessment
Give the child copymaster C96 (volume B) to complete.

LEVEL 5

Level Description

When constructing models and when drawing or using shapes, pupils measure and draw angles to the nearest degree, and use language associated with angle. They identify all the symmetries of 2-D shapes. They know the rough metric equivalents of Imperial units still in daily use and convert one metric unit to another. They make sensible estimates of a range of measures in relation to everyday situations.

TASK 14 — ACCURATE CONSTRUCTION OF 3-D MODELS A/B
C97-98

Resources
Card, glue, scissors, cartridge paper, protractors, rulers.

Organization
Children are required to work alone here but the model-making will have to be spread over several sessions.

What you do
In a number of different sessions, ask the child to construct each of the shapes listed on the copymaster. Use the copymaster as a record sheet for the child's work.

What the child does
The child constructs a number of 3-D shapes, measuring and drawing the angles correctly. This will take time and concentration and should therefore be done over a number of sessions.

Key question
Can the child construct shape models accurately?

Reassessment
Give the child a copy of C98. Ask them to keep this as a record of their model-making. The teacher will also need to check the work and initial the copymaster, which can be added to the pupil's profile.

TASK 15 — ANGLE LANGUAGE A/B
C99-100

Resources
None.

Organization
This is an individual task.

What you do
Give the child copymaster C99 to work on. If you require them to correctly spell the words without a prompt list, cut off the bottom of the copymaster so that the word list is omitted.

What the child does
The child has to fill in the angle vocabulary words in the appropriate places.

Key question
Can the child use language associated with angle?

Reassessment
Give the child copymaster C100 to complete.

TASK 16 — SHAPE PROPERTIES A/B
C101-102

Resources
None.

Organization
This is an individual task

What you do
This is intended as a catch-all task so give the child copymaster C101 and ask them to be as full as possible in their answers.

What the child does
The child has to demonstrate what they know by identifying and writing in what they know about the lines, angles and shapes on the copymaster.

Key question
Can the child demonstrate their knowledge of concepts and vocabulary about line, angle and shape?

Reassessment
Give the child copymaster C102 to work on.

TASK 17 — IMPERIAL/METRIC – MEASURES/ ESTIMATION A/B
C103-104

Resources
The packaging and items shown on the copymaster so that the child can determine measurements. These include a bag of sugar or sugar bag, a petrol can, a tape-measure, a milk bottle, a shampoo bottle, soap, a bag containing four apples.

Organization
This is an individual task.

What you do
Give the child access to the things listed on the copymaster

and a copy of C103. Discuss the child's estimates with them if it is necessary.

What the child does
The child enters imperial and metric measures, making conversions where necessary and makes estimates of measures.

Key question
Can the child convert imperial to metric measures and make sensible estimates?

Reassessment
Give the child access to all the things on the copymaster and a copy of copymaster C104 to work on. Resources required include a bag of flour or flour bag, a Thermos® flask, a school ruler, a soft-drink can, a washing-up liquid bottle, washing-powder, potatoes

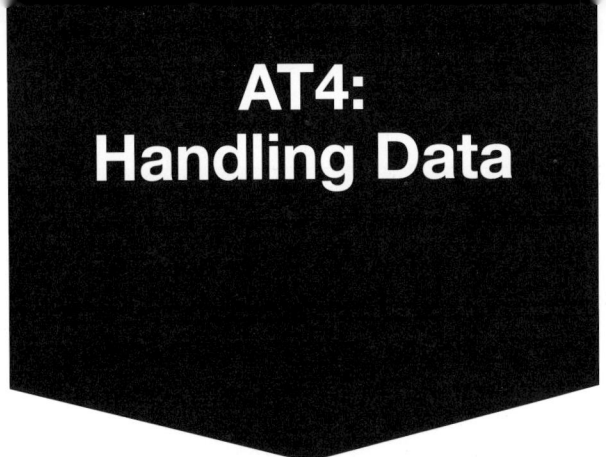

AT4: Handling Data

> **LEVEL 2**
>
> **Level Description**
>
> Pupils sort objects and classify them using more than one criterion. When they have gathered information, pupils record results in simple tables, block graphs and diagrams, in order to communicate their findings.

TASK 1 — SORTING OBJECTS A/B
C105-106

Resources
A range of packaging and items found in a cleaning cupboard. Beware of toxic substances. Include, for example, clean dusters, cloths, sponge, brush and dustpan, washing-up liquid, washing-powder, boot polish, and a collection of 2-D shapes which can be home-made from card or bought. Paper for the children to record results of their sorts.

Organization
This is an individual task but can be done by each child while they are a member of a group with the teacher looking on.

What you do
Observe the child while they sort the cleaning cupboard contents into sets and subsets using a variety of criteria. In another session or sessions use 2-D shapes as the collection for sorting. Use the copymaster as a record sheet for the child's work.

What the child does
The child has to do a series of sorts, using items commonly found in a cleaning cupboard and using a collection of 2-D shapes, while the teacher looks on. If the child is working in a group, you will have to ensure that each participant in the group has several tries and fully understands what he is doing.

Key question
Can the child sort things using more than one criterion?

Reassessment
Let the child do a variety of sorts using firstly a number of items found in a desk, and then some 3-D shapes. As resources, collect a variety of items found in or on a desk, including, for example, pens, pencils, stationery, postcards, stamps, blotter, pen tin, and a collection of 3-D shapes which can be empty packaging junk or a set of commercially produced shapes. Use copymaster C106 (sorting objects B) as a record of the child's achievements.

TASK 2 — GATHER INFORMATION/CONSTRUCT A TABLE A/B
C107-108

Resources
Other children to provide information, rough paper, squared paper, rulers.

Organization
The information-getting stage can be done in pairs or by small groups. Children should compile their own rough notes though and construct tables, without collaborating with one another, for submission.

What you do
Discuss with the children the instructions on the copymaster. Allow them to collect information and put it in tabular form.

What the child does
The child has to collect information, collate it and then tabulate it.

Key question
Can the child gather information and put it in a table?

Reassessment
Give the child copymaster C108 (gather information/construct table B) and proceed as for assessment A.

LEVEL 3

Level Description

Pupils extract and interpret information presented in simple tables and lists. They construct bar charts and pictograms, where the symbol represents a group of units, to communicate information they have gathered, and they interpret information presented to them in these forms.

TASK 3 — TABLE/LIST A/B
C109-110

Resources
None.

Organization
This task needs to be done individually.

What you do
Give the child copymaster C109 to complete.

What the child does
The child interprets and responds to the data on C109.

Key question
Can the child interpret tables and lists?

Reassessment
Give the child copymaster C110 to complete.

TASK 4 — BAR CHART/PICTOGRAM CONSTRUCTION A/B
C111-112

Resources
Rough paper, coins, children to provide information.

Organization
The getting of information can be done in pairs or by small groups but the information collation and presentation is an individual task.

What you do
Allow the child to collect and present the information.

What the child does
The child has to collect two sets of information by following the instructions on the copymaster, and then collate the information to create a bar chart and a pictogram.

Key question
Can the child construct bar charts and pictograms?

Reassessment
Give the child C112 and proceed as for assessment A. A pack of Happy Families cards, the school roll and the children's birth dates are required. If your school is very large, children could use the class lists for some of the classes.

TASK 5 — BAR CHART/PICTOGRAM INTERPRETATION A/B
C113-114

Resources
None.

Organization
This is an individual task but could be given to a whole class to do as a 'test'.

What you do
Give the child copymaster C113 to work on.

What the child does
The child has to interpret the charts on the copymaster.

Key question
Can the child interpret bar charts and pictograms?

Reassessment
Give the child copymaster C114 to work on.

Level Description

Pupils collect discrete data and record them using a frequency table. They understand and use the mode and median. They group data, where appropriate, in equal class intervals, represent collected data in frequency diagrams and interpret such diagrams. They construct and interpret simple line graphs. They understand and use simple vocabulary associated with probability, including 'fair', 'certain' and 'likely'.

TASK 6 — INTERPRET/CONSTRUCT FREQUENCY DIAGRAMS A/B
C115-116

Resources
Rough paper, children or adults to give information, depending on what the children decide to find out.

Organization
The interpretation part of the task is an individual effort. Children should work in pairs when constructing their diagrams, providing you can give them sufficient attention to ensure that in each pair both children are in command of what they are doing.

What you do
Give the child copymaster C115 to work on. For the last part of the task, discuss with the children the kind of data they may like to collect, and look in on what they are doing while they group the data they have collected. They can submit all their rough notes and the fair copy of a chart showing the collated results. It is appropriate to support them providing they understand fully what they are doing.

What the child does
The child has to respond to the data on the copymaster, and then decide on what data to collect. It may be personal details like how often children go to bed before 9 pm or preferences like how often children drink squash, fresh juice or fizzy drinks. They then have to collect information from a sample of their choosing and order and group the data in a chart.

Key question
Can the child interpret frequency diagrams, and collect and order discrete data in a frequency diagram?

Reassessment
Let the child have another try at working with frequency diagrams using copymaster C116 (interpret/construct frequency diagrams B).

TASK 7 — FREQUENCY DIAGRAMS – MEDIAN/MODE A/B
C117-118

Resources
Rough paper, graph paper, calculators if you think them appropriate.

Organization
This is an individual task.

What you do
Give the child copymaster C117. There is much work to be done here and you may wish the child to tackle the two tasks in separate sessions.

What the child does
The child has to interpret the data on the copymaster and draw a frequency chart and a bar-line graph.

Key question
Can the child draw a frequency chart and a bar-line graph, and do they know what the median and mode are?

Reassessment
Give the child copymaster C118 and proceed as for the assessment.

TASK 8 — 'LIKELIHOOD', 'EVENS' AND 'FAIR' A/B
C119-120

Resources
None.

Organization
This is an individual task to be done alongside the teacher.

What you do
Discuss all the challenges on the copymaster C119 with the child and use the copymaster to record all that the child achieves.

What the child does
The child has to demonstrate that they know about chance.

Key question
Can the child demonstrate an understanding of some words associated with probability?

Reassessment
Discuss the items on copymaster C120 ('likelihood', 'evens' and 'fair' B) with the child using the copymaster as a record sheet.

LEVEL 5

Level Description

Pupils understand and use the mean of discrete data. They compare two simple distributions, using the range and one of the measures of average. They interpret graphs and diagrams, including pie charts, and draw conclusions. They understand and use the probability scale from 0 to 1. Pupils find and justify probabilities, and approximations to these, by selecting and using methods based on equally likely outcomes and experimental evidence, as appropriate. They understand that different outcomes may result from repeating an experiment.

TASK 9 — MEAN AND RANGE A/B
C121-122

Resources
Calculators, rough paper.

Organization
This is an individual task.

What you do
Give the child the copymaster and a calculator if you wish.

What the child does
The child has to compute the mean and range of two sets of data.

Key question
Does the child know about the mean and range?

Reassessment
Give the child copymaster C122 to work on.

TASK 10 — CONSTRUCT/INTERPRET STATISTICAL DIAGRAMS A/B

C123-124

Resources
Rough paper, calculator.

Organization
This is an individual task.

What you do
Give the child copymaster C123 to work on.

What the child does
The children have to interpret the pie chart on the copymaster, construct pie charts and interpret the data to write reports.

Key question
Can the child interpret and construct a pie chart, and write a report on statistical data?

Reassessment
Give the child copymaster C124 to work on.

TASK 11 — ESTIMATE AND JUSTIFY PROBABILITIES A/B
C125-126

Resources
None.

Organization
This is an individual task and should be quick to do.

What you do
Give the child copymaster C125 to work on.

What the child does
The child has to demonstrate that they can use a probability scale by making entries on the copymaster and justifying them.

Key question
Can the child use a probability scale?

Reassessment
Give the child copymaster C126 (estimate and justify probabilities B) to work on.

TASK 12 — LISTING ALL POSSIBLE OUTCOMES A/B
C127-128

Resources
None.

Organization
This is an individual task.

What you do
Give the child copymaster C127 to work on.

What the child does
The child has to work out all possible outcomes on the copymaster.

Key question
Does the child understand how we can work out all possible outcomes of an event?

Reassessment
Ask the child to complete work on copymaster C128 (listing all possible outcomes B).

Name: _____ Date: _____

AT1 Level 2

A Select and talk about mathematics

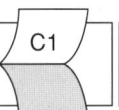

Talk about how you would find out these

 The cost of two cakes	 How many ice creams there will be
 How many children in school are having school dinner	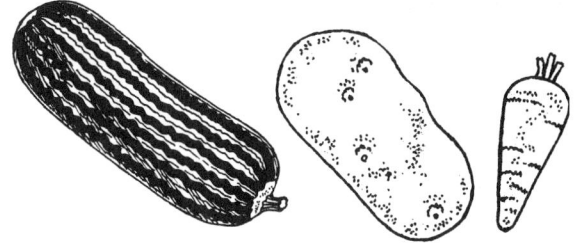 The heaviest vegetable
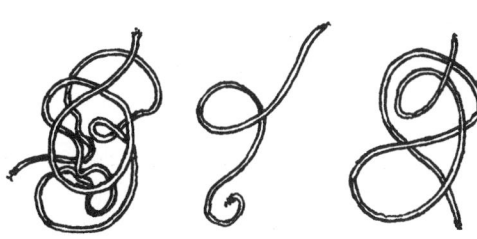 The longest piece of string	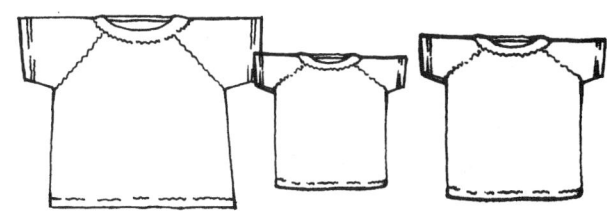 The biggest T-shirt
 The length of a skateboard track	 Sorting
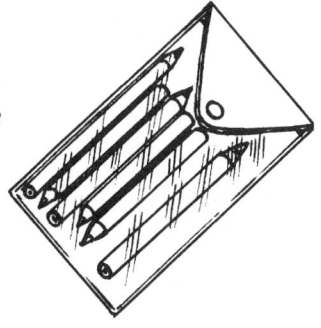 How many pencils will fill the case	 How many apples altogether

Name: _____ Date: _____   AT1 Level 2

B Select and talk about mathematics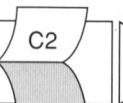

Talk about how you would find out these

The cost of two comics

How many sweets there are when some are eaten

How many children in school like swimming

The heaviest vegetable

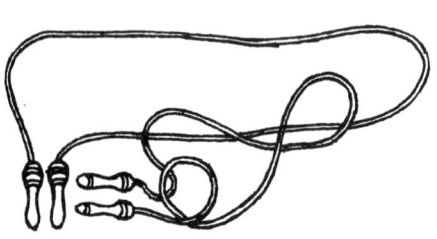

The longer skipping rope

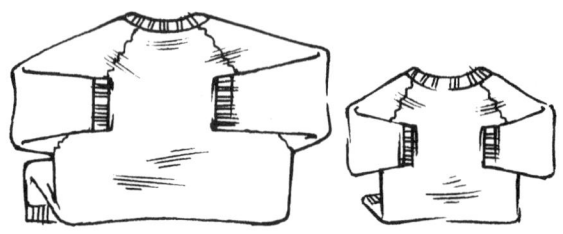

The bigger of two sweatshirts

The length of a jump

How many pairs of socks in the washing basket

How many in the box

Which parcel costs more to send

Name: _____ Date: _____

AT1 Level 2

A | **Mathematical language/diagram**   C3

Name of game   dominoes/snakes and ladders/ . . .

    Setting up .... ❏

    Rules of play .... ❏

    How to win .... ❏

    Mathematical language used

• •

In a pack of jelly beans there are
7 yellow ones, 4 pink ones, 2 black ones, 5 red ones, 6 green ones and 1 brown one

Put this information in a diagram

    Used block graph .... ❏

    Other .... ❏

7 yellow	5 red
4 pink	6 green
2 black	1 brown

Name: _____ Date: _____

AT1 Level 2

B | **Mathematical language/diagram**   C4

Name of game   beetle drive/bingo/ . . .

    Setting up .... ❏

    Rules of play .... ❏

    How to win .... ❏

    Mathematical language used

• •

In a pack of pocket toys there are
2 spinners, 4 badges, 6 mini monsters, 1 key ring, 5 stickers and 7 puzzles

Put this information in a diagram

    Used block graph .... ❏

    Other .... ❏

- -

2 spinners	1 key ring
4 badges	5 stickers
6 mini monsters	7 puzzles

Name: _____ Date: _____

AT1 Level 2

A | Respond to 'what if'

C5

What happens if two people sit on one side of a see-saw and three people sit on the other?

What happens to the length of a school week if you always have Friday off school?

A sweet shop sells toffee bars, chocolate bars and mint bars. What happens to sales of mint bars and chocolate bars if the shop sells out of toffee bars?

If you get into the dinner queue in single file instead of in pairs, what happens to the length of the queue?

If you can make 12 jam tarts with 100 g of flour, what happens to the number of tarts if you double the quantity of flour?

Dan and Di are doing ten sums each.
If Dan has done seven and Di eight, who is more likely to finish first?

There are 30 children in the class.
If ten children are away with flu, how many children will be marked present on the register?

Name: _____ Date: _____

AT1 Level 2

| B | Respond to 'what if' |

C6

What happens if there is a full bag of sugar on each side of a balance, and a second bag is added to one side of the balance?

What happens if your homework usually can be done before tea and then one day you are given twice the usual amount?

A café serves scones, chocolate cakes and flapjack. What happens to sales of scones and flapjack if the café sells out of chocolate cakes?

What happens to the length of your shoelace when you tie a bow in it?

If 100 g of flour makes 12 biscuits, what happens to the number of biscuits if you halve the amount of flour?

Stella gets all 16 of her calculations right. If Trisha does half of these, how many is that? What if Trisha gets two wrong? How many will she have done correctly?

There are 25 children in class. What if eight go on a trip? How many are in school?

Name: _____ Date: _____

AT1 Level 3

| A | Solve problems

C7

Career survey

Career choice

What I did

shopkeeper

nurse or doctor

teacher

scientist

Problems I had

dancer

engineer

actor

office worker

How I solved the problems

singer

bank manager

pilot

artist

 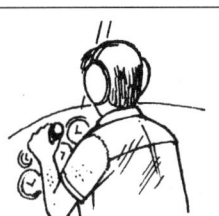

Name: _____ Date: _____

AT1 Level 3

B | Solve problems

C8

Art survey

What I did

Problems I had

How I solved the problems

Names of artists and number of votes

Name: _____ Date: _____

AT1 Level 3

| A | Organize, check, explain, use diagrams C9

Keep a record of all the television programmes you watch in one week

Write down the names of the days of the week and put the date on each day

Write down the name of each programme you see and how long it lasts

Copy your notes on to a chart

Present the chart to the class and tell them about it

Name: _____ Date: _____

AT1 Level 3

| B | Organize, check, explain, use diagrams   C10

Keep a record of what you eat at your main meal each day for a week
(It may be a school dinner or your evening meal)

Write down the names of the days of the week and put a date on each day

Write down exactly what you have to eat at your main meal each day

Copy your notes on to a chart

Show the chart to your teacher

Name: _____ Date: _____

A | Investigate a general statement

AT1 Level 3

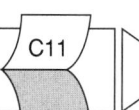

Test out this statement

In a set of dominoes, if we count the dots on each domino, there are more dominoes with seven dots than there are with ten dots

Do your rough notes here

Write your conclusion here

Name: _____ Date: _____

AT1 Level 3

B Investigate a general statement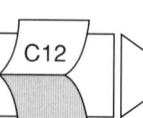

Test out this statement

All numbers that can be divided by 5 end in 5 or 0

Do your rough notes here

Write your conclusion here

Name: _____ Date: _____

AT1 Level 4

A Problem solving

C13

If you were going to give all the ceilings in school a coat of paint, write down

 **What** needs to be found out

 **How** the information is to be collected

 **What** has to be done with the information to arrive at an answer

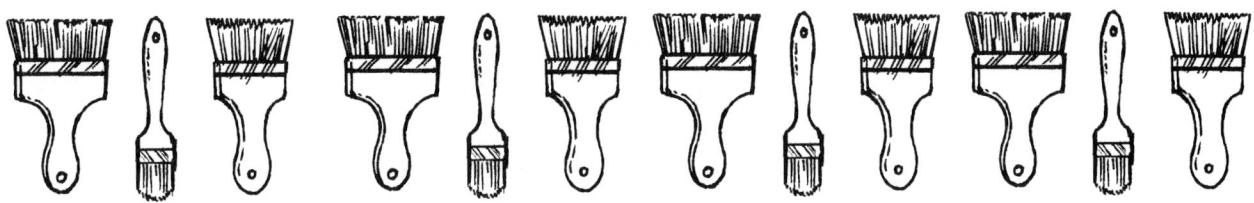

Name: _____ Date: _____

B | Problem solving

AT1 Level 4
C14

If you were going to find out how many books were in the school library, and what they were about, write down

 **What** needs to be found out

 **How** the information is to be collected

 **What** has to be done with the information to arrive at an answer

Name: _____ Date: _____

A | Present information/results clearly

AT1 Level 4
C15

Look at the ingredients in four different foods

Make a chart of your findings

Explain your work

Use this space for rough notes

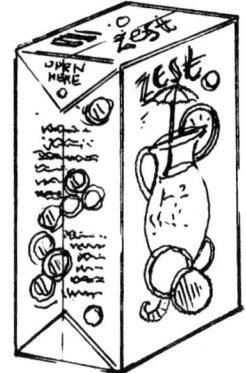

Name: _____ Date: _____

AT1 Level 4

B | **Present information/results clearly**

Make a timetable showing what happens in your class in a typical week

You can use pictures, words and symbols

The timetable should be easy to read at a glance
Explain your work

Use this space for rough notes

Let's see what I should be doing now

Name: _____ Date: _____

AT1 Level 4

| A | Pattern search – own ideas |

C17

square numbers	4	9							
triangular numbers	1	3							

Can you complete this table?

Look for a way of making each square number from triangular numbers

Write your notes and ideas here

Name: _____ Date: _____

AT1 Level 4

| B | Pattern search – own ideas

C18

Prime numbers up to 100 with the exception of 2 and 3 come before or after a multiple of which number (it is between 2 and 9)?

Write down here all your ideas about how to find this out

I think I have got some good ideas here

Name: _____ Date: _____

AT1 Level 5

C19

A Carry through a task

In the education supplement of a national newspaper an article about symmetry contained items on:

- Lewis Carroll's *Through the Looking Glass*
- Reflective and rotational symmetry
- The Vedic square
- Symmetry in letters, numerals and poems
- Handedness

Critically examine this range of topics as examples to demonstrate symmetry

Compile a list of topics you would include in such an article

This space is for rough notes

Name: _____   Date: _____

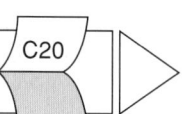

| B | Carry through a task |

What proportion of space do national newspapers devote to educational issues?

Choose a variety of newspapers.
Collect a number of issues of each and find out what their education coverage is

Write in rough

What you will do (in order)

What resources you need

How you will present your results

Name: _____ Date: _____

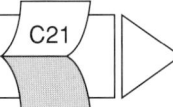

A | Use symbols etc in making diagrams

Library study
- Sit in the school library for an hour
- Write down how many children visit the library from which classes
- Put the information in a mathematical diagram

- Explain what kind of diagram it is and why you presented your results in this way

Spinner experiment

Colour spinner

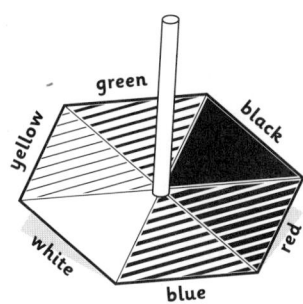

- Make a colour spinner
- Spin it 30 times
- Write down which colour the spinner rests on each time
- Put your results in a diagram

Name: _____ Date: _____

AT1 Level 5

| B | Use symbols etc in making diagrams | C22 |

School hall study
- List the classes in the school
- Choose a day of the week
- Ask each teacher how often their classes go into the hall on that day
- Write down what each teacher says
- Make a mathematical diagram

- Explain what kind of diagram it is and why you presented your results in this way

Die experiment

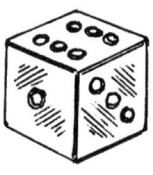

- Throw a die 30 times
- Write down which number is on top of the die each time
- Put your results on a diagram
- Explain what kind of diagram it is and why you presented your results in this way

Name: _____ Date: _____

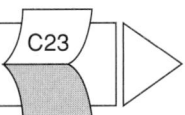

| A | Make/test generalizations |

Which television programmes are most popular among 10-year-olds? Test out your hypothesis

I think the following are the most popular programmes

This is how I will test it out

I shall present my results in these kinds of charts and diagrams

Conclusion

Name: _____ Date: _____

AT1 Level 5

B | Make/test generalizations　C24

Make a generalization about the hand spans of children of different ages. Test it out

My generalization is

I shall test this by

I shall present my results in these kinds of charts and diagrams

Conclusion

Name: _____ Date: _____

AT2 Level 2

A Add/subtract to 10; numbers to 100

C25

Write in the answers

3 + 3 = ☐   2 + 2 = ☐   7 − 5 = ☐

7 + 2 = ☐   1 + 7 = ☐   9 − 6 = ☐

1 + 5 = ☐   6 − 4 = ☐   2 − 1 = ☐

2 + 8 = ☐   3 − 2 = ☐   4 − 2 = ☐

....

Put the numbers in size order

17 36 98 4 23 57 61 49

☐ ☐ ☐ ☐ ☐ ☐ ☐ ☐

lowest   highest

11 85 2 92 76 27 14 4

☐ ☐ ☐ ☐ ☐ ☐ ☐ ☐

highest   lowest

....

Write in how many tens | Write in how many units

64 ☐ tens   94 ☐ tens   8 ☐ units   16 ☐ units

73 ☐ tens   47 ☐ tens   82 ☐ units   54 ☐ units

21 ☐ tens   12 ☐ tens   91 ☐ units   37 ☐ units

19 ☐ tens   39 ☐ tens   75 ☐ units   13 ☐ units

Name: _____ Date: _____

B | Add/subtract to 10; numbers to 100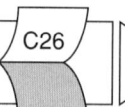

AT2 Level 2

Write in the answers

3 + 3 = ☐   2 + 2 = ☐   7 − 5 = ☐

7 + 2 = ☐   1 + 7 = ☐   9 − 6 = ☐

1 + 5 = ☐   6 − 4 = ☐   2 − 1 = ☐

2 + 8 = ☐   3 − 2 = ☐   4 − 2 = ☐

Put the numbers in size order

24   96   6   71   80   33   2   59

◯   ◯   ◯   ◯   ◯   ◯   ◯   ◯

lowest   highest

62   13   46   73   17   25   54   81

◯   ◯   ◯   ◯   ◯   ◯   ◯   ◯

highest   lowest

Write in how many tens | Write in how many units

71 ☐ tens   65 ☐ tens   11 ☐ units   38 ☐ units

84 ☐ tens   48 ☐ tens   27 ☐ units   51 ☐ units

19 ☐ tens   37 ☐ tens   43 ☐ units   34 ☐ units

23 ☐ tens   12 ☐ tens   99 ☐ units   67 ☐ units

Name: _____ Date: _____

AT2 Level 2

| A | Halves and quarters |

Join each number to half of that number

```
10                          1
     4                           5
6                                4
     2                           2
8                           3
```

Colour in half

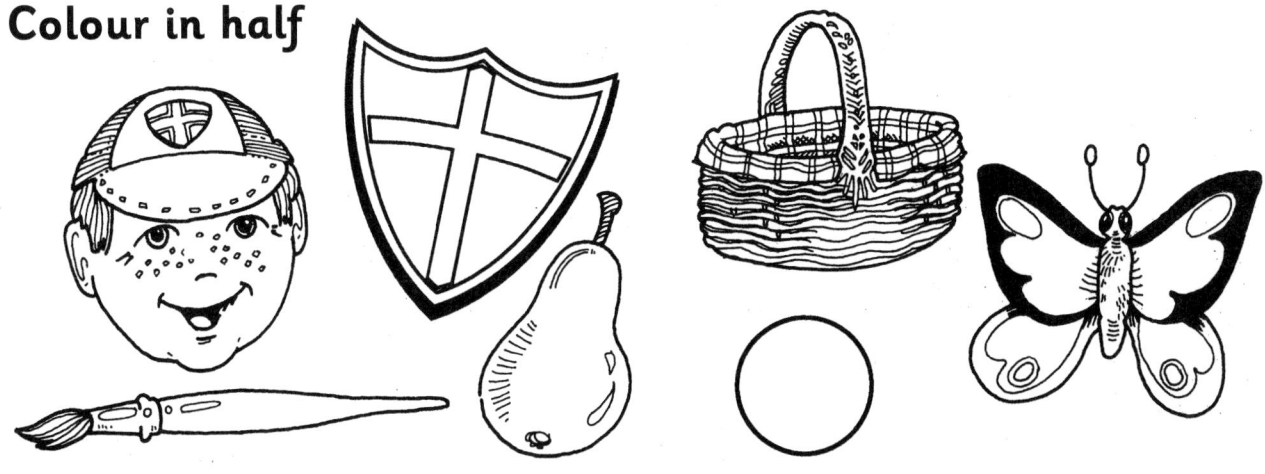

Colour to match (the whole with a quarter)

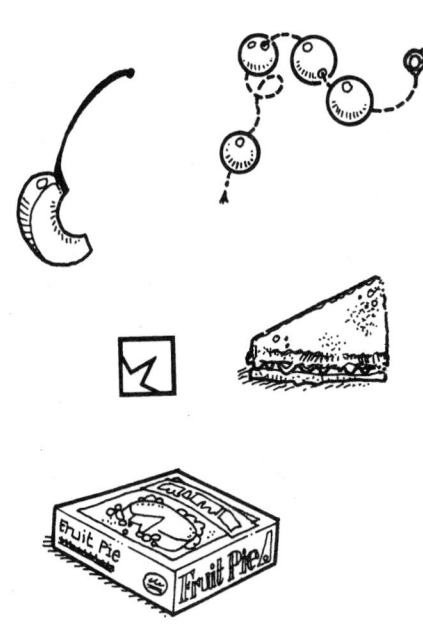

Name: _____ Date: _____

AT2 Level 2

| B | Halves and quarters |

C28

Join each number to half of that number

Draw half

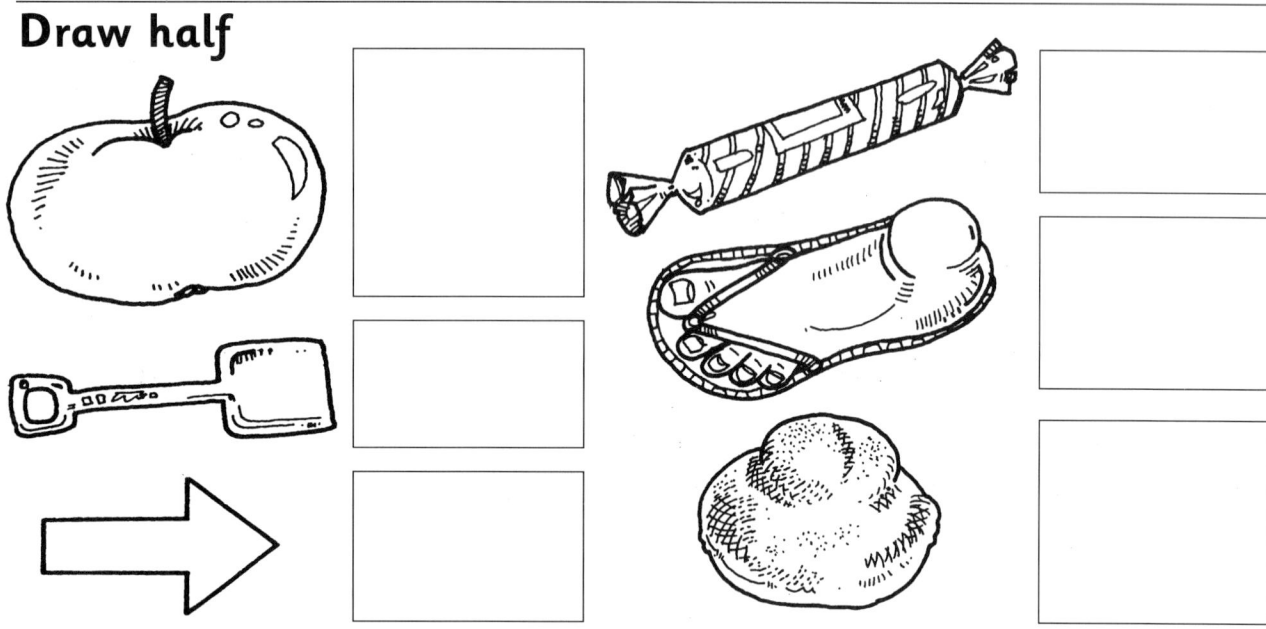

Colour to match (the whole with a quarter)

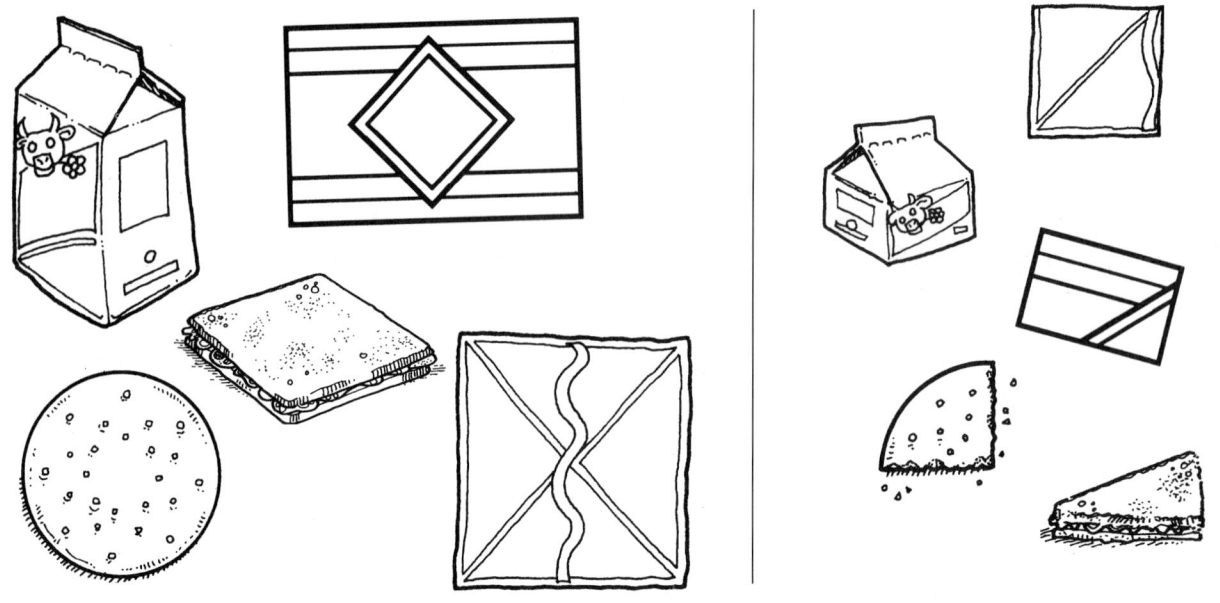

A | Number patterns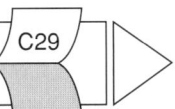

Complete these

5 + 0 = 5	10 − 6 = 4	7 + 0 = 7
4 + 1 = 5		6 + 1 = 7
0 + 5 = 5		
	4 − 0 = 4	

10 − 5 = 5	
9 − 4 = 5	6
8	5

Write down all the odd numbers that fit here

1 __ __ __ __ __ __ __ __ __ 19

Write down all the even numbers that fit here

2 __ __ __ __ __ __ __ __ __ 20

Name: _____ Date: _____

B | Number patterns

AT2 Level 2

Complete the number strings

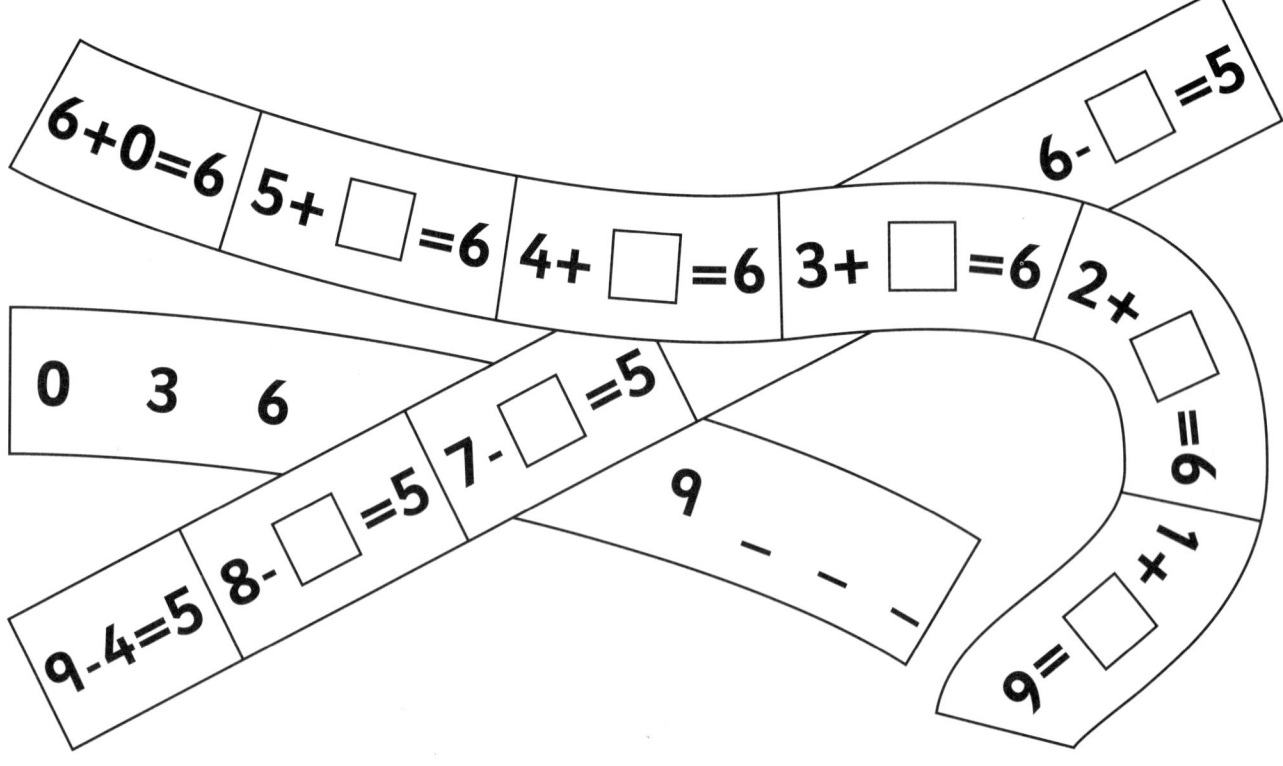

Colour the odd-numbered bingo balls in blue, and the even-numbered ones in red

Name: _____ Date: _____

AT2 Level 3

A | Interpreting big numbers

How many **10**s?

- (52 – 5 tens)
- (11)
- (88)
- (69)
- (43)
- (90)

What do the 7s in these numbers mean?
Are they hundreds, tens or units?

472 — [7] tens

57 — [ ] ___

702 — [ ] ___

175 — [ ] ___

17 — [ ] ___

798 — [ ] ___

Invent some numbers with

3 hundreds –	8 tens –	5 units –
9 hundreds –	4 tens –	2 units –
2 hundreds –	1 ten –	7 units –

Name: _____ Date: _____   AT2 Level 3

B Interpreting big numbers   C32

  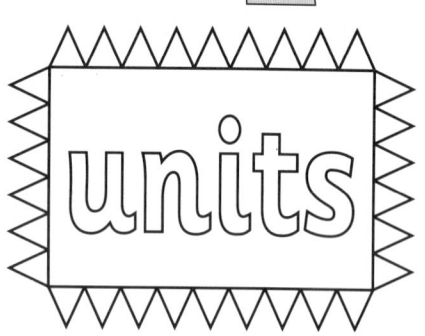

Write in how many tens

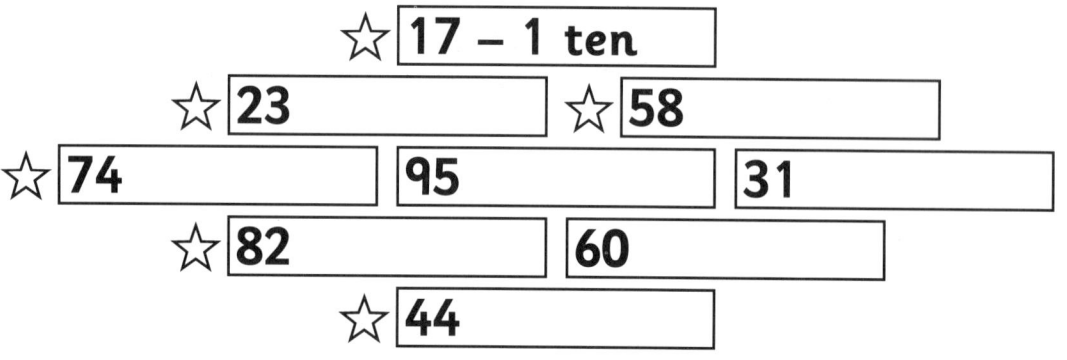

☆ 17 – 1 ten
☆ 23   ☆ 58
☆ 74   95   31
☆ 82   60
☆ 44

Write in how many hundreds

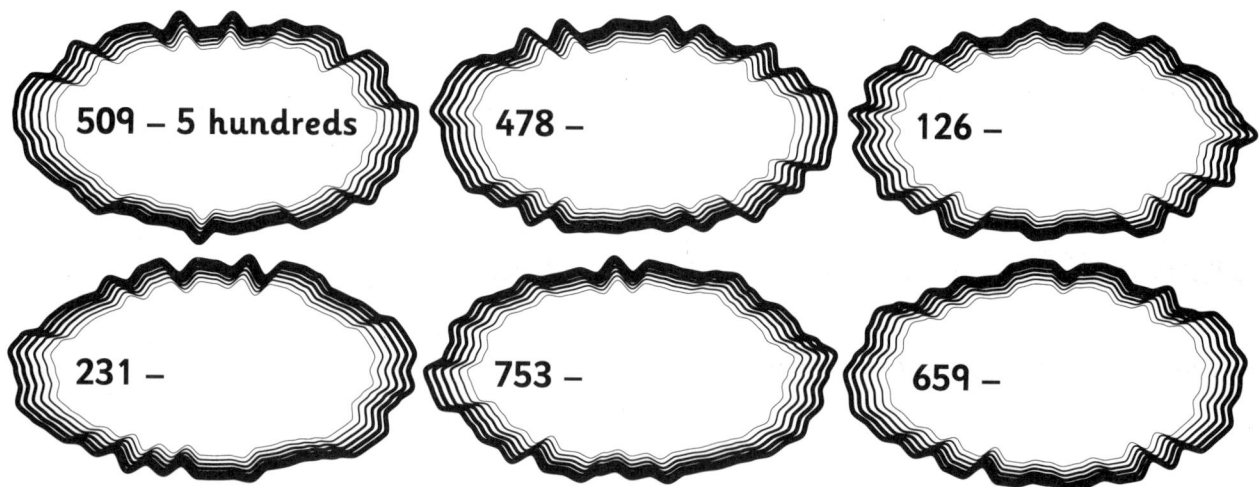

509 – 5 hundreds   478 –   126 –
231 –   753 –   659 –

What do the 3s in these numbers mean?
Are they hundreds, tens or units?

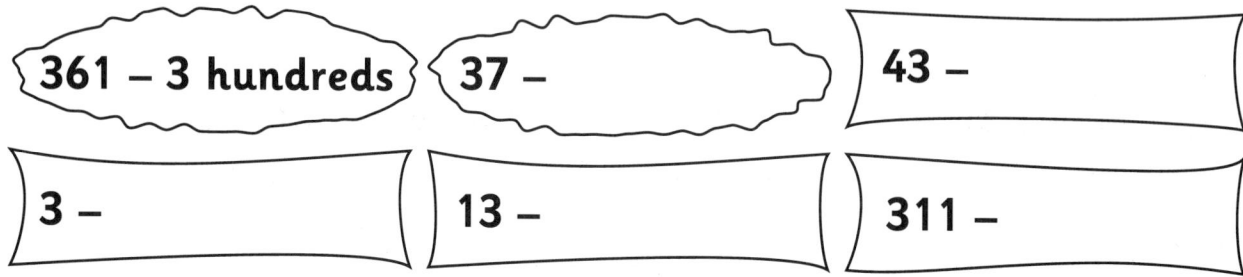

361 – 3 hundreds   37 –   43 –
3 –   13 –   311 –

Name: _____ Date: _____

AT2 Level 3

A Decimal money/approximation

C33

chocolate eggs 38p
milk chocolates £2.75
chocolate bear £3.15
mug with chocolates £2.50
chocolate rabbit £3.50
chocolate mints £1.99
selection box £1.69
orange creams £1.99

Totals Write in how much these cost

3 chocolate eggs ☐

2 selection boxes and 1 orange creams ☐

1 milk chocolates and 1 mug with chocolates ☐

2 chocolate mints and 1 chocolate egg ☐

2 chocolate bears ☐

2 chocolate rabbits ☐

Change Write in how much change from £10

4 selection boxes and 1 chocolate egg ☐ change

2 mugs with chocolates and 1 orange creams ☐ change

3 chocolate bears ☐ change

Approximation What are the approximate prices of these?

chocolate mints ☐   selection box ☐   chocolate egg ☐

Name: _____ Date: _____

AT2 Level 3

B | **Decimal money/approximation**

C34

pingbat 45p
hoopla £1.50
chess game £3.75
tennis racquet and ball £5.99
cricket bat and ball £6.69
football £8.99

Totals Write in how much these cost

3 pingbats ☐ 2 footballs ☐

2 hooplas and 1 chess game ☐ 1 tennis racquet and ball and 1 pingbat ☐

2 chess games and a cricket bat and ball ☐ 1 cricket bat and ball and 1 tennis racquet and ball ☐

Change Write in how much change from £15

1 cricket bat and ball and 1 chess game ☐ change

4 hooplas and 1 tennis racquet and ball ☐ change

1 football and 3 pingbats ☐ change

Approximation What are the approximate prices of these?

football ☐   cricket bat and ball ☐   tennis racquet and ball ☐

Name: _____ Date: _____

AT2 Level 3

A Negative numbers

Complete this subtraction square

−	1	2	3	4	5	6	7	8	9	10
1										
2										
3										
4										
5										
6										
7										
8										
9										
10										

Function Mouse

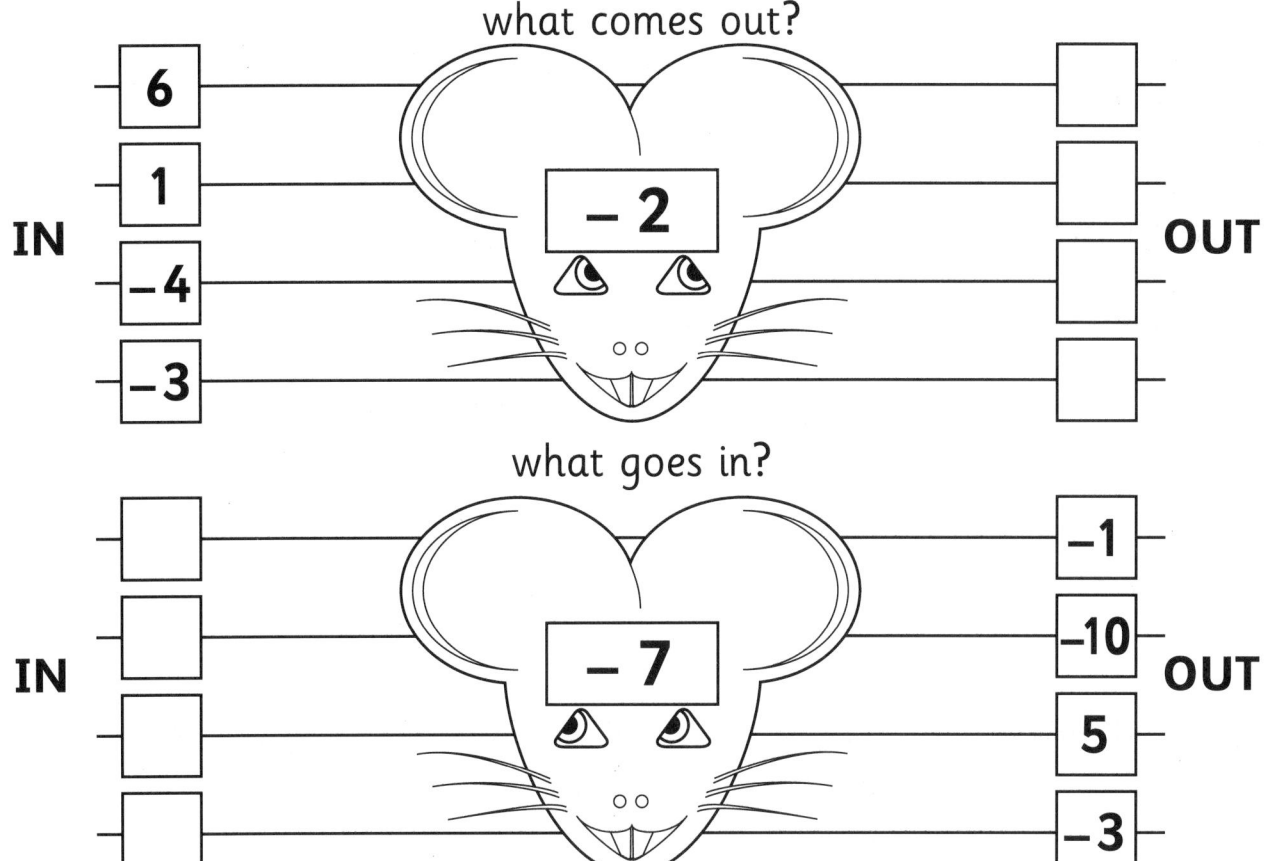

Name: _____ Date: _____

B | Negative numbers

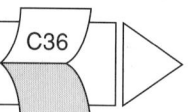

Complete this subtraction square

−	2	4	6	8	10	12	14	16	18	20
2										
4										
6										
8										
10										
12										
14										
16										
18										
20										

Number Chomper

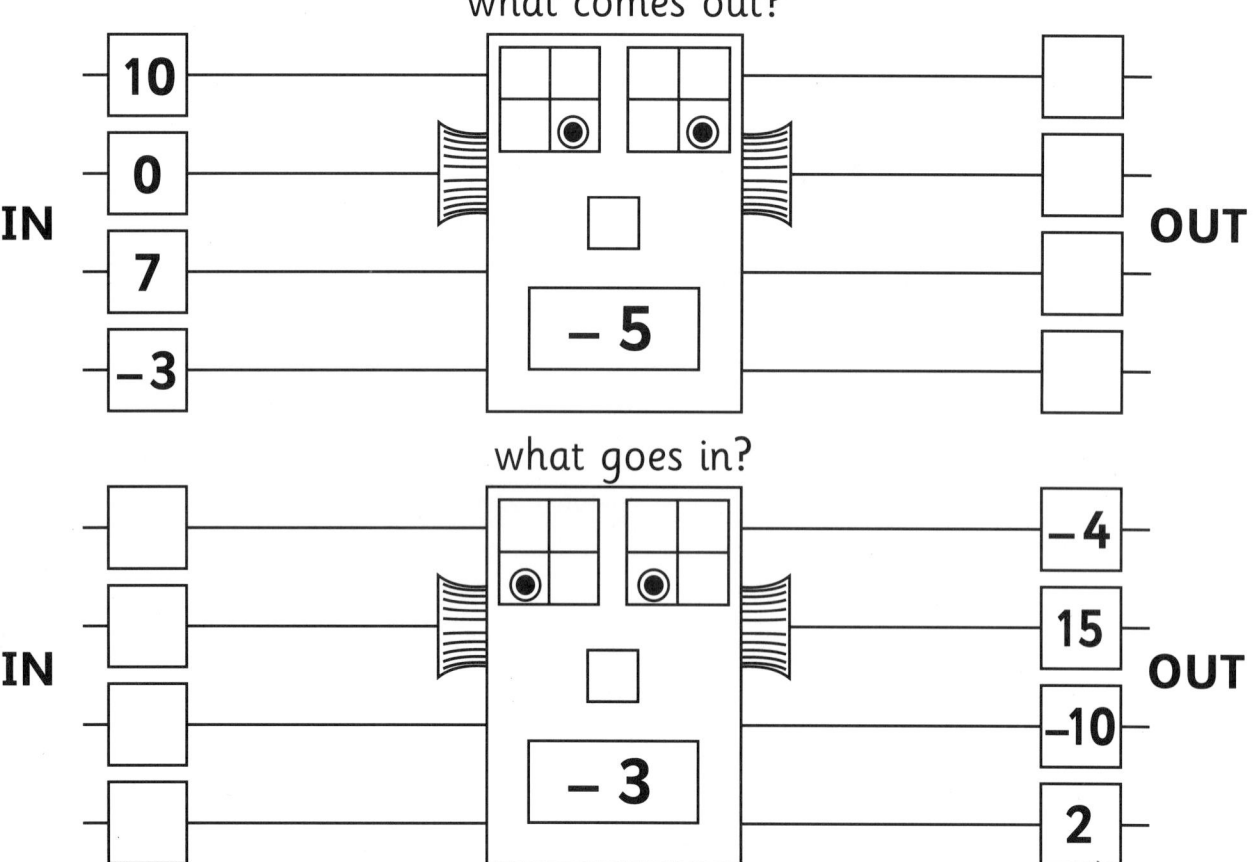

Name: _____ Date: _____

AT2 Level 3

A | Add/subtract to 20 including 0

12 + 5 =

16 + 2 =

11 + 6 =

18 + 1 =

17 + 1 =

15 + 4 =

10 + 3 =

14 − 0 =

16 − 4 =

12 − 1 =

11 − 2 =

20 − 0 =

18 − 9 =

14 − 9 =

---

15 +   = 18

16 +   = 17

12 +   = 18

19 +   = 20

10 +   = 19

13 +   = 15

16 +   = 20

20 −   = 12

14 −   = 10

15 −   = 9

17 −   = 15

19 −   = 11

12 −   = 10

17 −   = 12

  + 15 = 18

  + 14 = 16

  + 10 = 20

  + 12 = 17

  + 17 = 19

  + 11 = 12

  + 13 = 15

  − 2 = 13

  − 8 = 10

  − 0 = 14

  − 6 = 11

  − 3 = 18

  − 1 = 19

  − 4 = 17

Name: _____ Date: _____

AT2 Level 3

B | **Add/subtract to 20 including 0**

C38

18 + 0 =

16 + 2 =

15 + 3 =

12 + 5 =

10 + 6 =

13 + 4 =

10 + 3 =

13 − 0 =

14 − 4 =

12 − 2 =

19 − 0 =

18 − 8 =

17 − 6 =

14 − 9 =

11 + ___ = 15

13 + ___ = 17

10 + ___ = 19

20 + ___ = 20

12 + ___ = 18

17 + ___ = 19

14 + ___ = 14

16 − ___ = 12

14 − ___ = 13

12 − ___ = 10

19 − ___ = 17

17 − ___ = 14

13 − ___ = 11

15 − ___ = 15

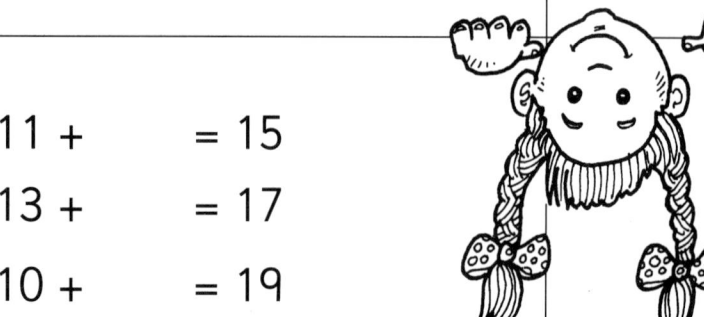

___ + 11 = 18

___ + 18 = 20

___ + 14 = 16

___ + 15 = 19

___ + 19 = 20

___ + 12 = 20

___ + 13 = 17

___ − 1 = 19

___ − 4 = 12

___ − 2 = 14

___ − 5 = 13

___ − 6 = 11

___ − 0 = 17

___ − 9 = 10

Name: _____ Date: _____

A | **2, 5, 10 × tables and up to 5 × 5**　　　AT2 Level 3　C39

2 × table	5 × table	10 × table

16 legs on ☐ giraffes

☐ legs on 3 giraffes

3 cost ☐ p

5 cost ☐ p

☐ corners on 1 table

20 corners on ☐ tables

☐ musicians in 1 trio

6 musicians in ☐ trios

Name: _____   Date: _____

AT2 Level 3

B | 2, 5, 10 × tables and up to 5 × 5

C40

2 × table	5 × table	10 × table

☐ wheels on 1 tricycle

18 wheels on ☐ tricycles

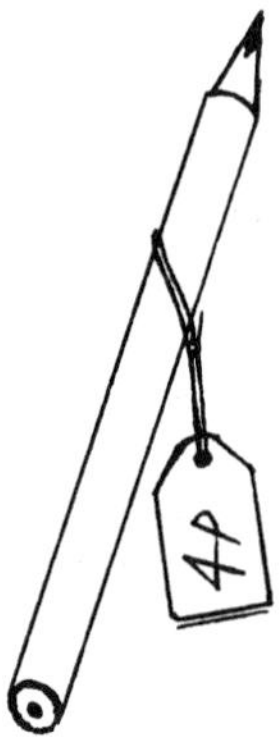

5 cost ☐ p

2 cost ☐ p

☐ legs on 3 horses

20 legs on ☐ horses

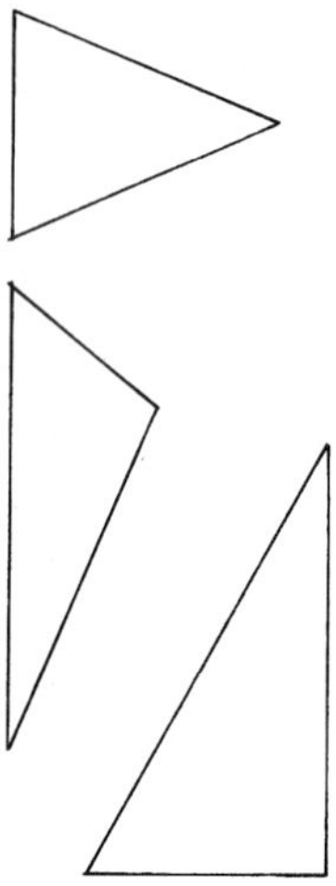

3 triangles have ☐ sides

15 sides on ☐ triangles

Name: _____ Date: _____   AT2 Level 3

| A | Multiplication/division problems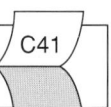

How many ways can these stickers be put into equal piles?

....

How much do 4 of each of these posters cost?

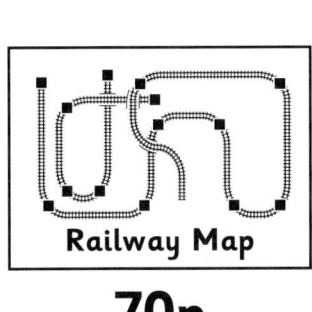

4 cost _____   4 cost _____   4 cost _____

How many of each could you buy with £4

£4 buys _____   £4 buys _____   £4 buys _____

....

Which ways can these pens be shared?
(giving equal shares and none left over)

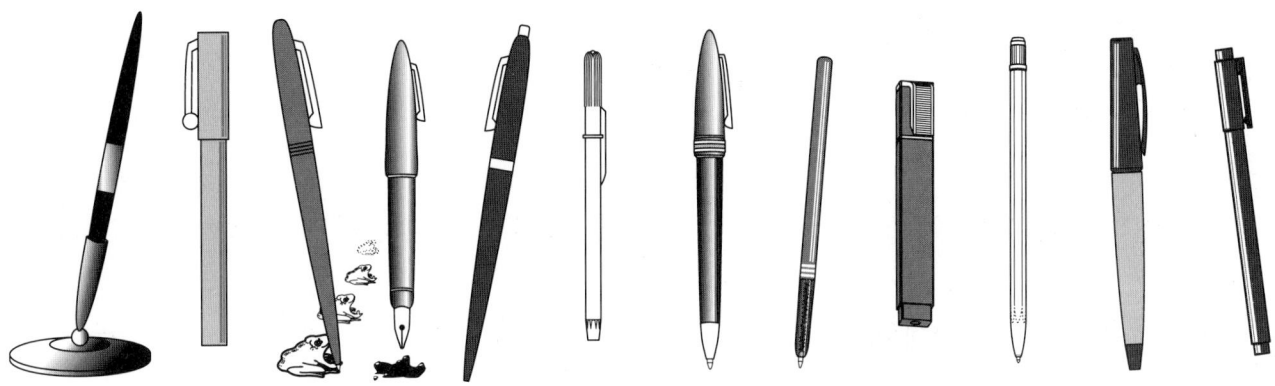

Name: _____ Date: _____

B Multiplication/division problems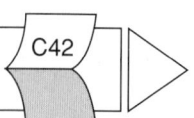

How many ways can these books be put into equal piles?

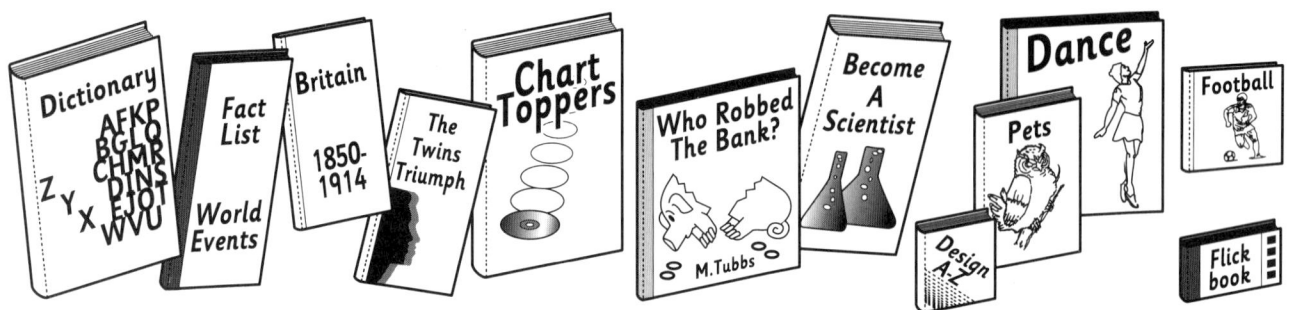

How much do 3 of each of these LPs, CDs and tapes cost?

 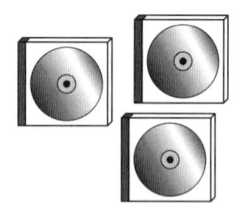 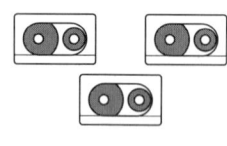

LPs £5.25 each   **CDs £12.50 each**   **Tapes £1.99 each**

3 cost _____   3 cost _____   3 cost _____

How many of each could you buy with £20

£20 buys _____   £20 buys _____   £20 buys _____

Which ways can these notebooks be shared?
(giving equal shares and none left over)

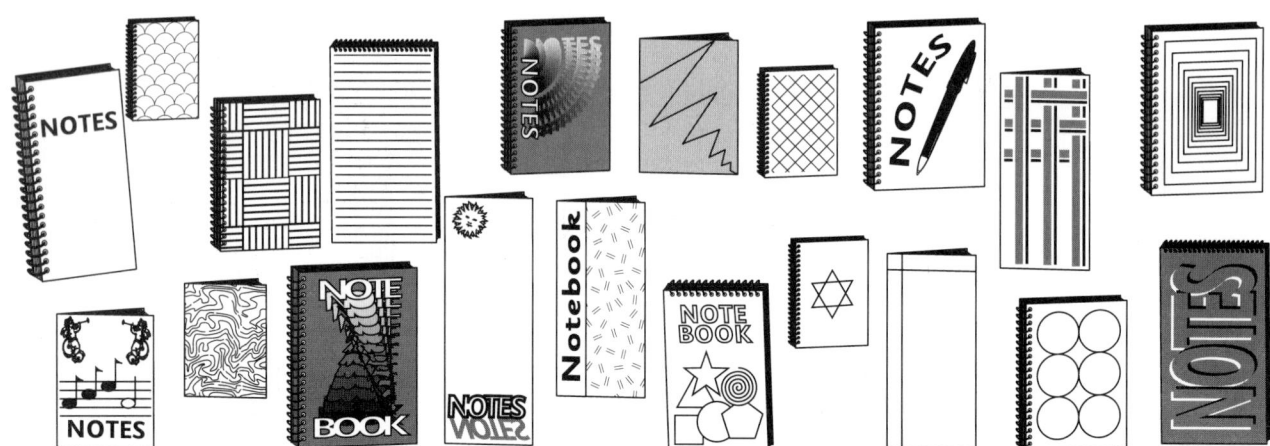

Name: _____ Date: _____ AT2 Level 3

A | Remainders

Write in the remainder

6 ÷ 5 = 1 remainder ☐   20 ÷ 3 = 6 remainder ☐

7 ÷ 4 = 1 remainder ☐   25 ÷ 10 = 2 remainder ☐

• •

What are the answers here?

Put 'r' for remainder

15 ÷ 2 =   3 ÷ 2 =

18 ÷ 7 =   10 ÷ 4 =

9 ÷ 2 =   14 ÷ 6 =

17 ÷ 5 =   4 ÷ 3 =

11 ÷ 10 =   12 ÷ 5 =

8 ÷ 3 =   5 ÷ 2 =

Can you do these lying down? Only kidding!

Name: _____ Date: _____

AT2 Level 3

B | Remainders

C44

What are the answers here?
Put 'r' for remainder

13 ÷ 6 =   18 ÷ 7 =

16 ÷ 5 =   23 ÷ 8 =

6 ÷ 4 =   4 ÷ 3 =

19 ÷ 10 =   21 ÷ 5 =

8 ÷ 3 =   11 ÷ 4 =

22 ÷ 5 =   24 ÷ 7 =

....

Write in the remainder

6 ÷ 5 = 1 remainder ☐

7 ÷ 4 = 1 remainder ☐

20 ÷ 3 = 6 remainder ☐

25 ÷ 10 = 2 remainder ☐

Can you do these upside down? Only kidding!

Name: _____ Date: _____

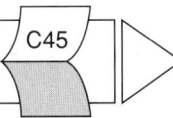

AT2 Level 3

A | Patterns and computation strategies

Complete the patterns

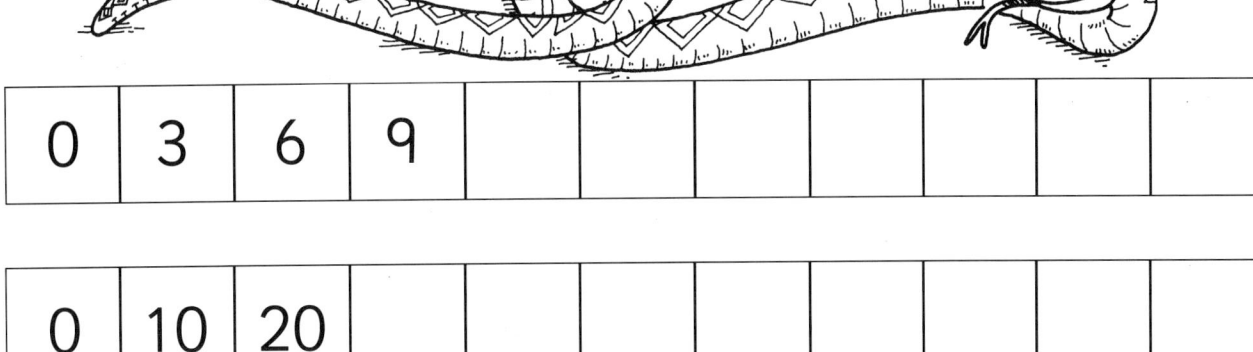

| 0 | 3 | 6 | 9 | | | | | | | |

| 0 | 10 | 20 | | | | | | | | |

| 15 | 20 | | | | | | 55 | 60 | |

| | | 28 | 30 | 32 | 34 | | | | |

| 17 | | | 23 | | | 29 | | | |

Write down what you do to work out these

67 + 21   43 − 21

Name: _____ Date: _____

B | Patterns and computation strategies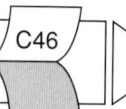

Complete the patterns

0, 5, 10, ◯, ◯, ◯, ◯

1, 3, 5, ◯, ◯, ◯, ◯

30, 35, 40, ◯, ◯, ◯, ◯

◯, ◯, ◯, 16, 18, ◯, ◯

◯, ◯, 30, 40, 50, ◯, ◯

Write down what you do to work out these

67 + 21   43 − 21

AT2 Level 4

Name: _____ Date: _____

C47

A Place value

Write down

These numbers multiplied by 10

76
302
11
555
37
0·2

These numbers multiplied by 100

4
30
66
0·9
48
12

....

Write these numbers in numerals having divided them by 10

Four thousand three hundred and two

One thousand nine hundred and seventy-six

Nine thousand and eleven

....

Write these numbers in numerals having divided them by 100

Five thousand two hundred and sixteen

Four thousand four hundred and forty-four

B Place value

Write these numbers in numerals having divided them by 10

Six thousand seven hundred and eighty-nine ☐

One thousand seven hundred and twenty-one ☐

· ·

Write these numbers in numerals having divided them by 100

Nine thousand and four ☐

Two thousand six hundred and thirty-seven ☐

· ·

×10		×100	
0·4		5	
311		0·10	
17		432	
679		77	
58		121	
715		56	

AT2 Level 4

Name: _____ Date: _____

A | Computation

C49

Addition

| 352 + 114 | 620 + 279 | 432 + 379 | 504 + 486 | 264 + 578 |

Subtraction

| 763 − 172 | 936 − 751 | 642 − 430 | 501 − 367 | 222 − 103 |

Multiplication

| 17 × 7 | 43 × 4 | 71 × 8 | 65 × 3 | 50 × 2 |

Division

| 7)21 | 8)37 | 2)88 | 4)90 | 5)36 |

Decimals

| 5·05 + 6·22 | 7·33 + 8·05 | 42·01 − 2·65 | 57·21 − 33·10 |

Mental Arithmetic

Answers	Mark
1.	
2.	
3.	
4.	
5.	
6.	
7.	
8.	
9.	
10.	
11.	
12.	
13.	
14.	
15.	

Name: _____ Date: _____

AT2 Level 4

| B | Computation | C50 |

Addition

| 694 + | 350 + | 456 + | 199 + | 462 + |
| 171 | 326 | 274 | 304 | 339 |

Subtraction

| 956 − | 411 − | 298 − | 874 − | 364 − |
| 463 | 209 | 143 | 672 | 189 |

Multiplication

| 38 × | 25 × | 94 × | 43 × | 36 × |
| 8 | 9 | 3 | 7 | 2 |

Division

6)47   5)63   3)99   9)71   2)11

Decimals

| 71·11 + | 9·86 + | 59·71 − | 37·34 − |
| 5·38 | 27·65 | 11·90 | 29·50 |

Mental Arithmetic

Answers	Mark
1.	
2.	
3.	
4.	
5.	
6.	
7.	
8.	
9.	
10.	
11.	
12.	
13.	
14.	
15.	

Name: _____ Date: _____

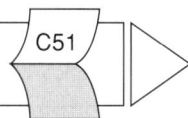

A | Calculator problems

Use a calculator to help you to solve these
Give your answers to two decimal places where appropriate

How many chairs will fit across the school hall?

How many books are borrowed from your school library by children aged between 9 and 11 years old on a day when 50% of 9-year-olds and 25% of 10- and 11-year-olds change their books?

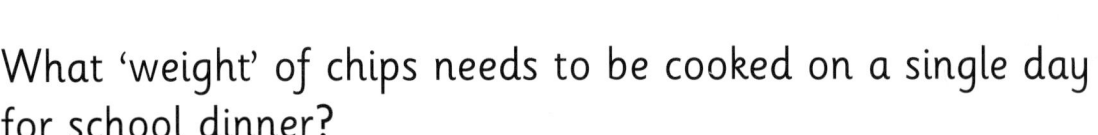

What 'weight' of chips needs to be cooked on a single day for school dinner?

Name: _____   Date: _____

B | Calculator problems

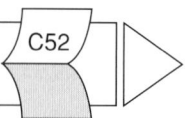

Use a calculator to help you to solve these
Give your answers to two decimal places where appropriate

How many hours of lesson time are there in a school year?

A roof tile covers an area of 10 x 10 cm.
How many tiles would be needed to put a roof
on a school extension if the new roof area is 20.24 x 18.67 m?

The soap dispensers in school washrooms pour out
1.05 ml of liquid soap each time they are used.
If they are used 19,762 times, how many litres of
liquid soap are needed?

Name: _____ Date: _____

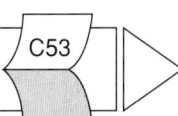

| A | Fractions and percentages |

What fractions are these? Write

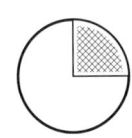 ☐

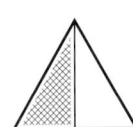 ☐

6 (of 48) ☐

1 (of 100) ☐

 ☐

What are the answers to these? Write or draw

$\frac{1}{4}$ of 16 ☐

$\frac{1}{6}$ of  ☐

$\frac{1}{12}$ of  ☐

$\frac{1}{6}$ of 36 ☐

$\frac{2}{3}$ of 90 ☐

Write what these are as percentages

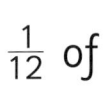 _____ %

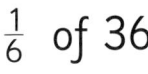 _____ %

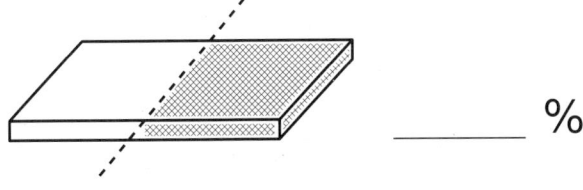

_____ %

Draw these

33% of a string of six sausages

10% of a 10 cm ruler

50% of a cake

Name: _____ Date: _____

AT2 Level 4

B Fractions and percentages

C54

What fractions are these? Write

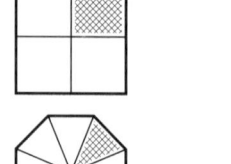 ☐

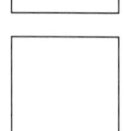 ☐

7 (of 21) ☐

10 (of 100) ☐

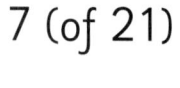 ☐

What are the answers to these? Write or draw

$\frac{1}{4}$ of 20 ☐

$\frac{1}{8}$ of 64 ☐

$\frac{3}{17}$ of 49 ☐

$\frac{1}{3}$ of 3 ☐

$\frac{2}{5}$ of  ☐

Write what these are as percentages

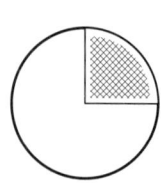 ____ %

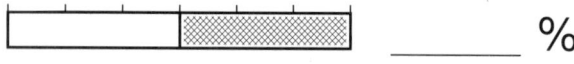 ____ %

 ____ %

Draw these

20% of a 10 cm ruler

50% of a currant bun

75% of an apple

Name: _____ Date: _____

AT2 Level 4

A | Patterns, multiples, factors, squares

Here is a tree diagram for 6.

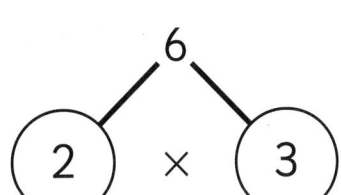

Draw trees for

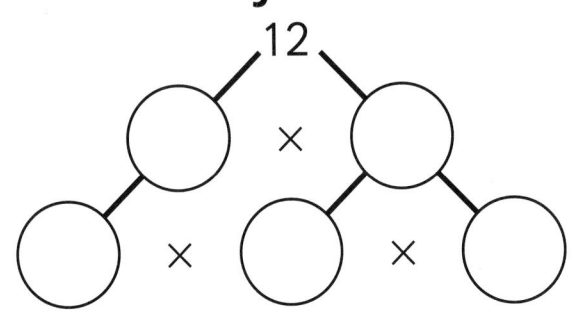

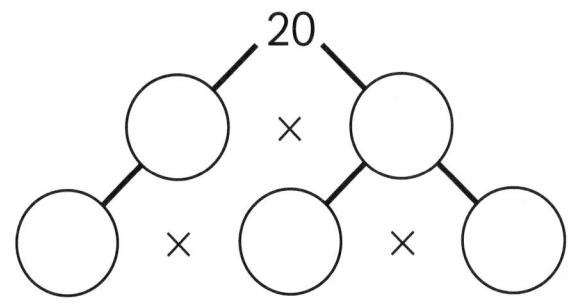

Solve these

$2^2 =$ ☐ $16 = ☐^2$

$3^2 =$ ☐ $49 = ☐^2$

$6^2 =$ ☐ $81 = ☐^2$

$8^2 =$ ☐ $121 = ☐^2$

I think I'm a square!

List all the prime numbers between 1 and 51

1 51

Name: _____ Date: _____

AT2 Level 4

B | Patterns, multiples, factors, squares

C56

Here are the 'roots' or factors of 6

2 and **3**

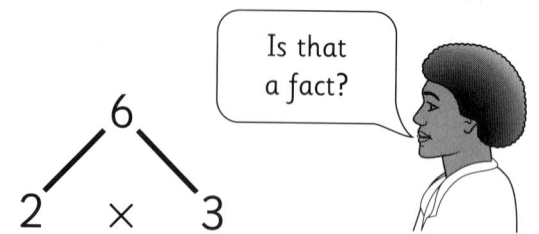

Find the factors of

15

24

Solve these

4^2 = ☐ 4 = ☐^{2}

5^2 = ☐ 64 = ☐^{2}

7^2 = ☐ 144 = ☐^{2}

10^2 = ☐ 16 = ☐^{2}

Find the primes

51	52	53	54	55	56	57	58	59	60
61	62	63	64	65	66	67	68	69	70
71	72	73	74	75	76	77	78	79	80
81	82	83	84	85	86	87	88	89	90
91	92	93	94	95	96	97	98	99	100

Colour in all the prime numbers here

A | Formulae/equations in words

Choose a number between one and a hundred

Double it – add ten – divide by two – take away four – take away your number

What is the answer? ☐   Now try another number

What can you say about each answer?

....

If I halve a number, multiply it by 10, take away 3 and get 57, what did I start with?

Starting number

☐

....

Write down what is happening in these number sequences

21, 31, 41 → 211, 311, 411

5, 6, 7, 8 → 25, 36, 49, 64

436, 272, 160 → 386, 222, 110

Name: _____ Date: _____

B | Formulae/equations in words

AT2 Level 4

C58

Choose a number between two and ten
Treble it and take away five. What do you get?
Try some other numbers

Answers to trials

Number chosen ☐ ☐ ☐ ☐ ☐

Answer number ☐ ☐ ☐ ☐ ☐

···

"If I add 10 to a number and then multiply it by 2 and take away 7 and end up with 15, what was my starting number?"

☐ **Starting number**

···

Write down what is happening in these number sequences

5, 6, 7, 8 → 50, 60, 70, 80

144, 132, 120, 108 → 12, 11, 10, 9

3, 6, 9, 12, 15 → 6, 9, 12, 15, 18

Name: _____ Date: _____

AT2 Level 4

| A | Coordinates in the first quadrant

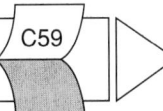

Plot the points marking the corners of a quadrilateral on the squared paper above

        1, 3   6, 5   8, 7   2, 10

Join up the points

Now draw another quadrilateral in red and write down the coordinates of its corners here

Name: _____ Date: _____

AT2 Level 4

B | Coordinates in the first quadrant   C60

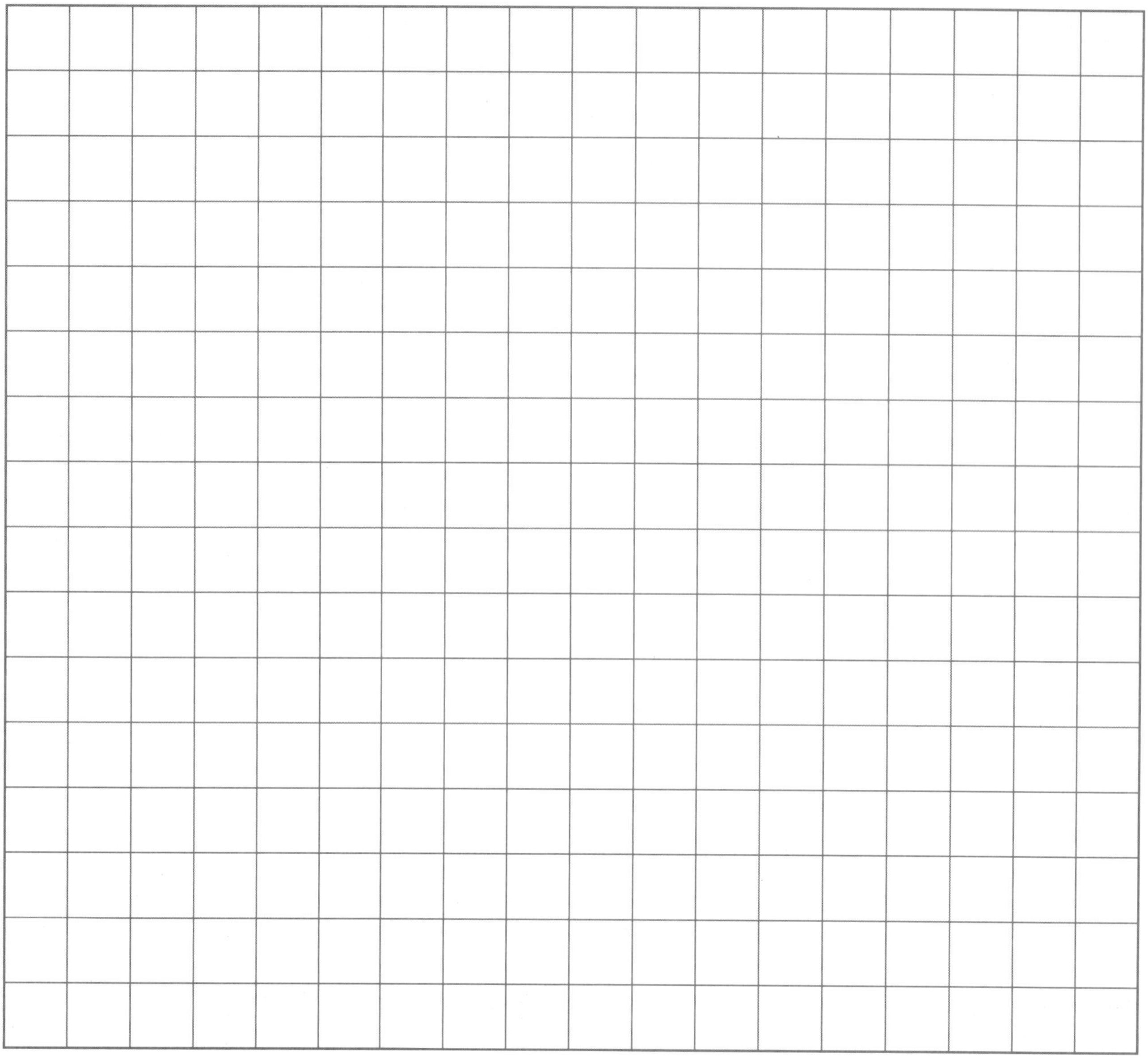

Plot the points marking the corners of a triangle on the squared paper above

2, 2   7, 5   3, 9

Join up the points

Now draw another triangle in red and write down the coordinates of its corners here

| A | Multiply/divide by 10, 100 and 1,000 |

Multiply by 10

- 9
- 99
- 72·4
- 657·01

Divide by 10

- 27
- 180
- 9·76
- 0·15

Multiply by 100

- 339
- 4,270
- 44·3
- 389·76

Divide by 100

- 7
- 11
- 31·2
- 0·9365

Multiply by 1,000

- 47
- 327
- 68·34
- 0·547

Divide by 1,000

- 22
- 5,963
- 0·754
- 998·728

B | **Multiply/divide by 10, 100 and 1,000** | AT2 Level 5 | C62

Multiply by 10

66	☐	0.2	☐
13	☐	0.02	☐

Divide by 10

793	☐	17·7	☐
2	☐	3·42	☐
44	☐	551·76	☐

Multiply by 100

31	☐	1·5	☐
5,744	☐	60·05	☐

Divide by 100

899	☐	92·7	☐
59	☐	333·33	☐

Multiply by 1,000

4	☐	0·01	☐
17	☐	99·973	☐

Divide by 1,000

55	☐	4·215	☐

Name: _____ Date: _____

AT2 Level 5

A Negative numbers/decimals

C63

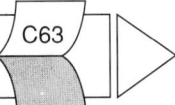

Solve these

+ 16 + + 11 ☐   + 1 − + 6 ☐

+ 7 + − 2 ☐   + 15 − − 2 ☐

+ 3 + − 12 ☐   − 13 − + 5 ☐

− 10 + − 4 ☐   − 14 − − 8 ☐

I'm positive about these negative numbers!

Now try these

0·21 + 23·25 ☐   97·20 − 56·12 ☐

7·78 + 31·41 ☐   19·26 − 0·45 ☐

9·21 + 3·43 ☐   120·34 − 20·43 ☐

11·6 + 91·11 ☐   0·41 − 0·11 ☐

93·33 × 40·15 ☐   13·27 ÷ 2·48 ☐

137·12 × 0·11 ☐   304·12 ÷ 23·83 ☐

5·23 × 41·23 ☐   723·11 ÷ 52·25 ☐

146·33 × 0·03 ☐   0·25 ÷ 0·12 ☐

AT2 Level 5

B Negative numbers/decimals

Solve these

+10 + +5 ☐   +3 − +5 ☐

+8 + −2 ☐   +1 − −9 ☐

−6 + +4 ☐   −14 − +16 ☐

−7 + −4 ☐   −15 − −2 ☐

Did you find four of the answers are negative numbers!

Now try these

0·07 + 3·32 ☐   0·41 − 0·17 ☐

138·45 + 8·92 ☐   975·38 − 25·83 ☐

38·27 + 4·14 ☐   3,840·43 − 596·7 ☐

341·53 + 81·73 ☐   83·59 − 63·06 ☐

820·33 × 54·55 ☐   386·73 ÷ 45·03 ☐

8·77 × 8·78 ☐   446·34 ÷ 22·64 ☐

0·86 × 0·038 ☐   4·90 ÷ 0·85 ☐

66·72 × 8·76 ☐   174·31 ÷ 11·02 ☐

AT2 Level 5

A Fractions and percentages

C65

1 1.25 kg of play dough makes 15 play bread rolls

How much is needed to make 18 rolls? ☐

How many g make 1 roll? ☐

2 Rewrite the following report using percentages instead of fractions

Half ☐ of all 10-year-olds have a pet of their own.

Three-quarters ☐ of those own a dog. The leading

brand of dog food 'Doggo' is bought by two-thirds ☐

of 10-year-old dog-owners. Only one twelfth ☐ of

owners have a black dog.

Five-eighths ☐ of all dogs have a short name.

Only one in 210 dogs looks like its owner.

3 Convert these percentages into fractions

25% = ☐   33·33% = ☐

5% = ☐   60% = ☐

4 Solve these

30% of 3 kg ☐   60% of 1,000 gallons ☐

$\frac{1}{4}$ of 200 girls ☐ $\frac{2}{3}$ of 540 dinners ☐

Name: _____ Date: _____

AT2 Level 5

B Fractions and percentages

C66

1 It takes 500 ml of shampoo to wash the hair of 36 children

How much does each child need? ☐

How much shampoo would be needed to wash the hair of 24 children? ☐

2 Rewrite the following using percentages instead of fractions

Three-quarters ☐ of all 11-year-olds have a bike.

One-third ☐ of the bikes are mountain bikes.

Two-thirds ☐ of 11-year-old bike-owners spend money on biking accessories. One owner in six ☐ has a red bike. Seven-eighths ☐ of bike-owners have a cycling helmet. One in 230 owners check their brakes before they ride their bikes.

3 Convert these percentages into fractions

40% = ☐   66·66% = ☐

10% = ☐   75% = ☐

4 Solve these

30% of 1 litre ☐   50% of 12·26 g ☐

$\frac{1}{6}$ of a class of 36 children ☐

$\frac{1}{12}$ of 888 raffle tickets ☐

Name: _____ Date: _____

AT2 Level 5

A Multiply and divide

Solve these without using a calculator

621 × 47 =

302 × 59 =

484 × 71 =

561 × 84 =

219 × 36 =

Seating in a school hall can be in rows of 15 or 12 (with a centre aisle).
What are the two best ways of seating 300 people?

There are 675 bedding plants on order at the garden centre.
How can they best be arranged in 45 containers?

Cartons of cereal are packed in containers of 32.
How many containers are needed for 506 cartons?

Name: _____ Date: _____

AT2 Level 5

B | Multiply and divide

C68

Solve these without using a calculator

594 × 87 ☐

219 × 93 ☐

372 × 65 ☐

438 × 74 ☐

145 × 58 ☐

• •

Seating in a theatre comes in 12-seat units.
What are the ways 1,500 seats can be arranged? The maximum capacity is 45 rows. Remember there can be one or two aisles.

☐

• •

The holiday shop receives 892 sticks of rock.
They can be laid in cartons of 35 or 50.
Which arrangement would leave fewest loose sticks?
Work this out using cartons of the same size and then using a mix of cartons of different sizes.

Name: _____ Date: _____

AT2 Level 5

A | Formulae and equations

C69

 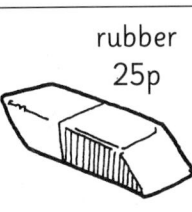    

pencil top 12p | rubber 25p | pencil sharpener 58p | pencil 18p | giant clips 22p | stapler 99p

6   4   3   2   9   2

Write in the cost of all these numbers of items, using
c = cost and n = number of items. **T** = total cost ($T = cn$)

name of item	number bought	cost of each	T = cn	T

Here are the dimensions of some rectangles.
Calculate their perimeters using the equation $p = 2(a + b)$.

a	dimensions b	perimeter (p)
33 cm	10 cm	
22 m	9 m	
19·2 mm	11·3 mm	
16·05 cm	43·2 cm	
760·1 m	229·7 m	

Name: _____ Date: _____

AT2 Level 5

B | Formulae and equations

C70

 key-ring 50p |  ghost 13p |  beetle 6p |  cat model 67p |  purse 99p |  badge 35p

3   5   7   6   2   4

Write in the cost of all these numbers of items, using **c** = cost and **n** = number of items. **T** = total cost (T = cn)

name of item	number bought	cost of each	T = cn	T

Explore Euler's relation (F + V = E + 2) where F = number of faces, V = number of vertices and E = number of edges.

name of shape	number of vertices	number of sides	number of edges	F + V = E + 2

Name: _____ Date: _____

AT3 Level 2

| A | Names of 2-D, 3-D shapes | C71 |

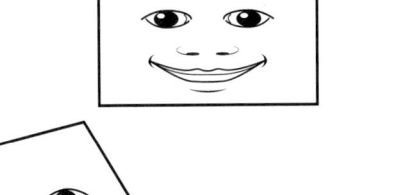
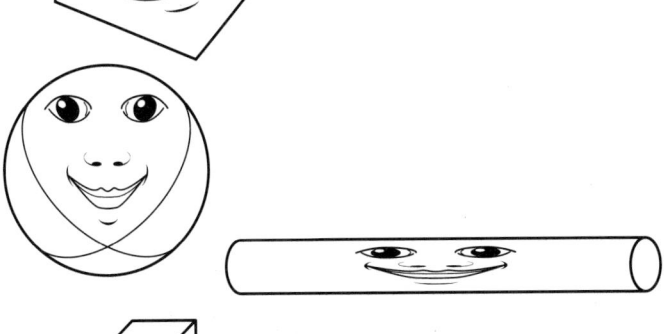

cuboid faces _____
corners _____

circle

triangle sides _____

sphere

hexagon sides _____

cylinder

rectangle sides _____
corners _____

cube faces _____
corners _____

pentagon sides _____

square corners _____
sides _____

B — Names of 2-D, 3-D shapes

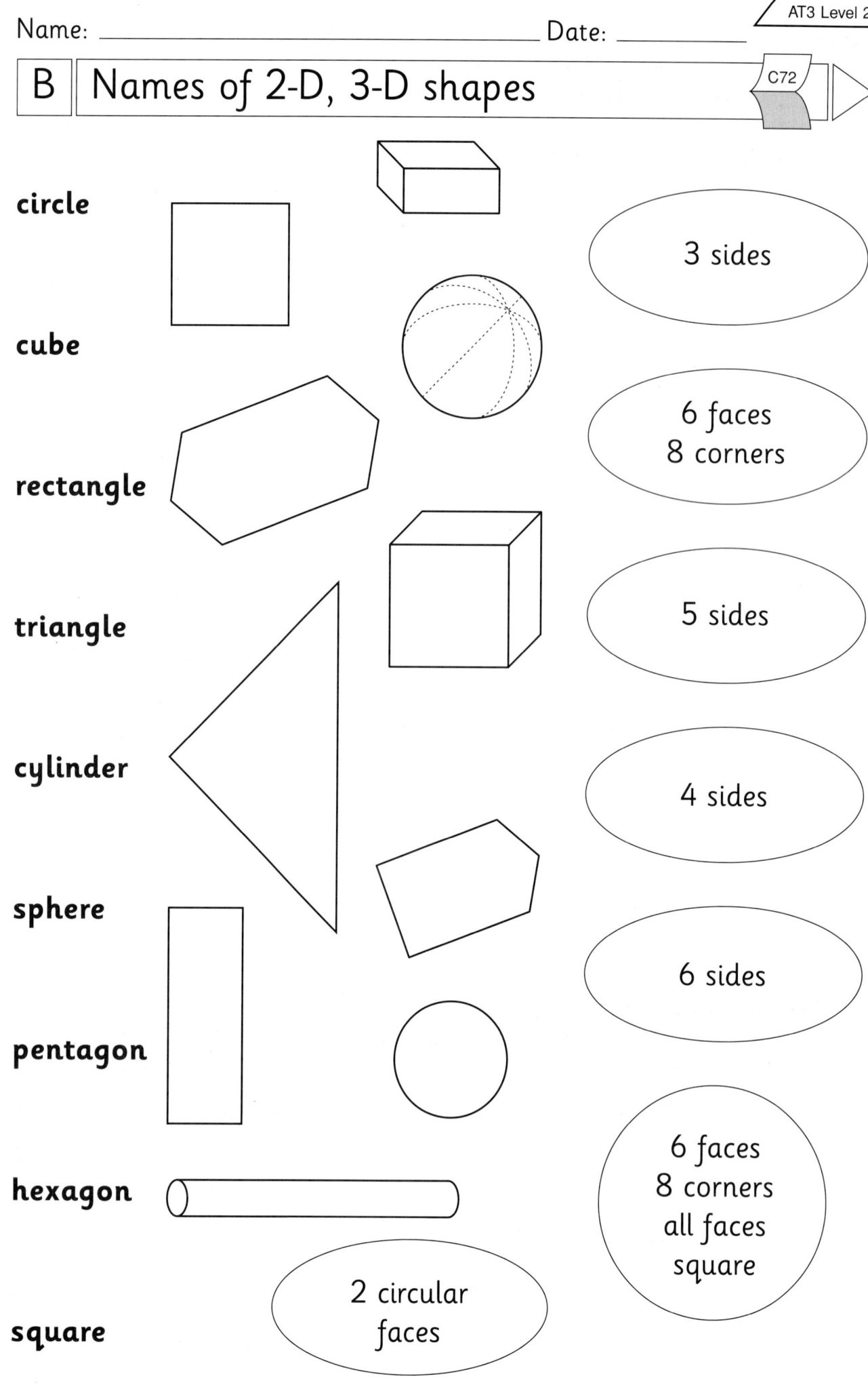

circle

cube

rectangle

triangle

cylinder

sphere

pentagon

hexagon

square

3 sides

6 faces
8 corners

5 sides

4 sides

6 sides

6 faces
8 corners
all faces
square

2 circular
faces

Name: _____ Date: _____

AT3 Level 2

C73

A | Types of movement

MOVEMENT LESSON RECORD

Theme: computer game

Session 1   **Rules of the game**
                Can move whole body in straight lines (translation) ....❏
                Can turn whole body (use body to 'map out' game) ....❏

Session 2   **Developing moves**
                Turning through right angles
                (use body to trace entire 'game field') ....❏

Session 3   **Playing to win**
                Mobilize parts of the body to show angles and turns
                (invent detailed rules eg escape, select, pick up using angles
                of arm, leg, body)..................❏

Name: _____ Date: _____

AT3 Level 2

| B | Types of movement

C74

MOVEMENT LESSON RECORD

Theme: space experience

Session 1   The mission begins
              Can move whole body in straight lines (translation) .... ❑
              Can rotate whole body working either as astronaut or
                as spacecraft .... ❑

Session 2   In space, planet exploration
              Can turn whole body through a right angle .... ❑
              Can repeat turning through 1, 2, 3, 4 right angles .... ❑

Session 3   Mission accomplished
              Can mobilize parts of body to show angles, turns, including
                right and left .... ❑

Name: _____ Date: _____

A Right angles

C75 AT3 Level 2

Draw ⌐ where you see right angles

| B | Right angles |

Draw ⌐ where you see right angles

Name: _____ Date: _____

AT3 Level 2

| A | Measure (NSU and SU) length/mass |

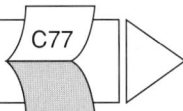

Draw in what you measured using these

span	cubit
pace	foot
stride	things for weighing

....

Name some things you could measure using these units

metre	kilogram
yard	pound
centimetre	gram
mile	ounce

Name: _____ Date: _____

AT3 Level 2

| B | Measure (NSU and SU) length/mass |

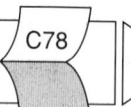

Do some measuring with these

span	
cubit	
foot	
pace	
stride	
⚖	

Talk about what you measure

. . . .

Join up to show which units you would use for these measuring jobs

kilogram

gram

ounce

pound

metre

centimetre

mile

yard

curtain material

pears

washing line

height

journey distance

margin

Name: _____ Date: _____

AT3 Level 3

A | Sorting shapes

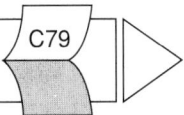

Using bought-in geometric shapes and mathematically accurate 3-D shapes, sorts are done according to criteria

Sort	Explanation given/notes
1	
2	
3	
4	
5	

Can identify criteria used in sorts done by the teacher or other children

Sort	Criteria discussed/notes
1	
2	
3	
4	
5	

Name: _____ Date: _____

AT3 Level 3

B | Sorting shapes

C80

Using card shapes and packaging/junk, sorts are done according to criteria

Sort	Explanation given/notes
1	
2	
3	
4	
5	

Can identify criteria used in sorts done by the teacher or other children

Sort	Criteria discussed/notes
1	
2	
3	
4	
5	

Name: _____ Date: _____

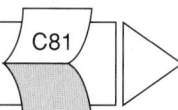
AT3 Level 3

A Reflective symmetry

Put a ring round the pictures that show reflective symmetry

Name: ______________________ Date: __________

AT3 Level 3

C82

B | Reflective symmetry

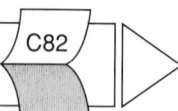

Put a ring round the pictures that show reflective symmetry

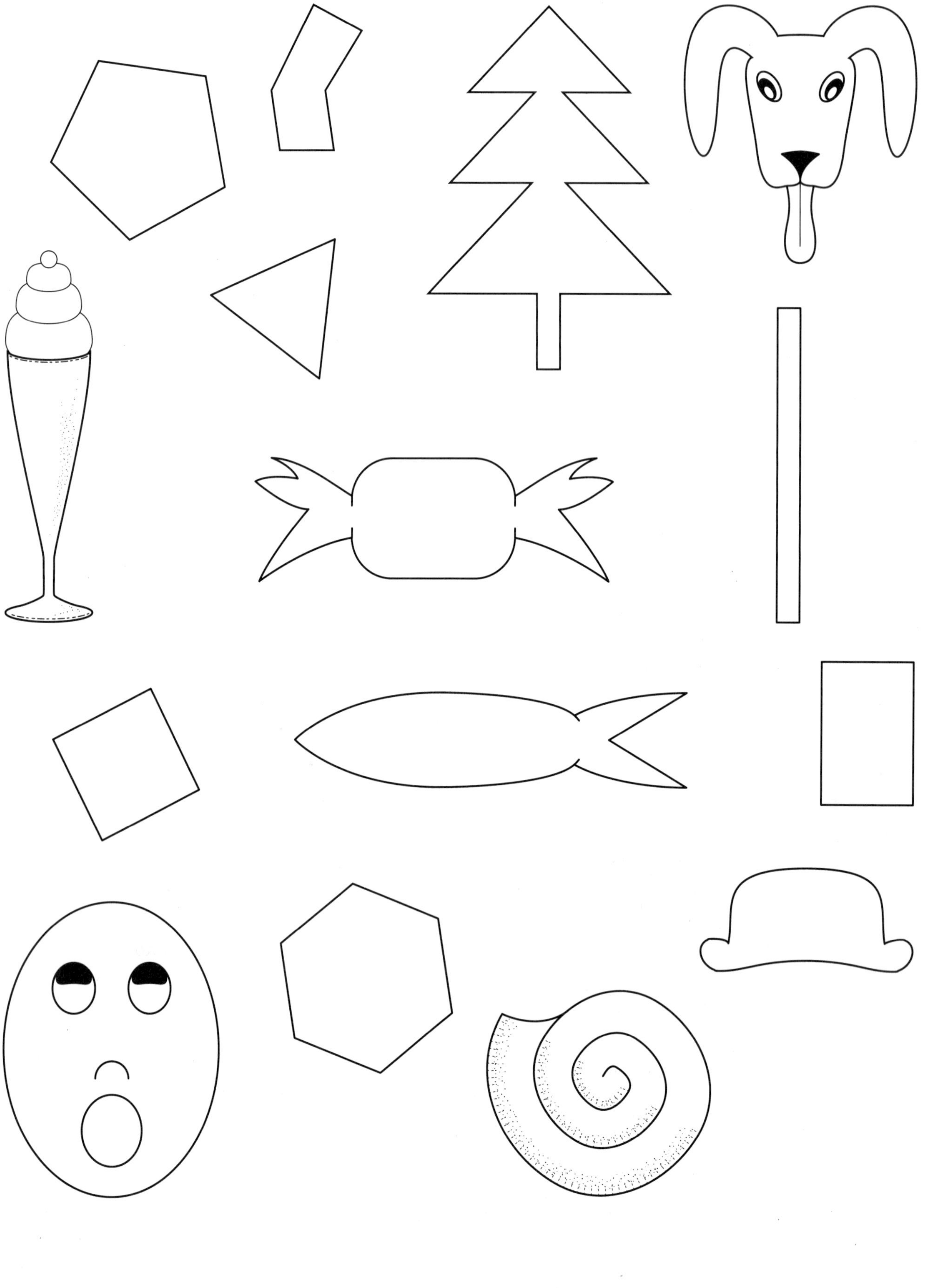

Name: _____ Date: _____   AT3 Level 3

A Measure length/capacity/mass/time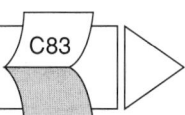

Measure each of these using an appropriate non-standard unit and again using metric units; or minutes and seconds

		non-standard unit	metric
length	Length of a notice board		
	Length of a calculator		
capacity	How much a paper cup holds		
	How much a drinking straw holds		
weight	The 'weight' of a loaf of bread		
	The 'weight' of a box of crayons		
time	How long it takes to do the class register		minutes/seconds
	How long it takes to run round the playground		minutes/seconds

Name: _____ Date: _____

B | **Measure length/capacity/mass/time**

AT3 Level 3

C84

Measure each of these using an appropriate non-standard unit and again using metric units; or minutes and seconds

		non-standard unit	metric
length	Length of a pen 		
length	Height of your teacher 		
capacity	How much a flower vase holds 		
capacity	How much an eggcup holds 		
weight	The 'weight' of a bag of potatoes 		
weight	The 'weight' of a pair of gloves 		
time	How long it takes to write your full name ten times 		minutes/seconds
time	How long it takes to get changed for games 		minutes/seconds

Name: _____ Date: _____

AT3 Level 4

A | Construct 2-D/3-D shapes; reflection

C85

TEACHER'S RECORD

Can construct	Trial	Success
square		
rectangle		
circle		
net for cube		
net for cuboid		
net for pyramid		
net for prism		
Can reflect shapes in a mirror line		
Remarks		

Name: _____ Date: _____   AT3 Level 4

B | **Construct 2-D/3-D shapes; reflection**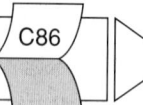

Put a ring around these tasks as you try them
Colour them in when you are successful

Construct a square	**Construct a rectangle**
Construct a circle	
Draw a net for a cube	**Draw a net for a cuboid**
Draw a net for a pyramid	**Draw a net for a prism**
Reflect shapes in a mirror line	

A Congruence

Draw lines to join the shapes that are congruent and write the word congruent along each line

Name: _____ Date: _____

AT3 Level 4

| B | Congruence |

C88

Draw lines to join the shapes that are congruent and write the word congruent along each line

Name: _____ Date: _____

AT3 Level 4

A Rotational symmetry

These shapes show rotational symmetry
Complete the pictures

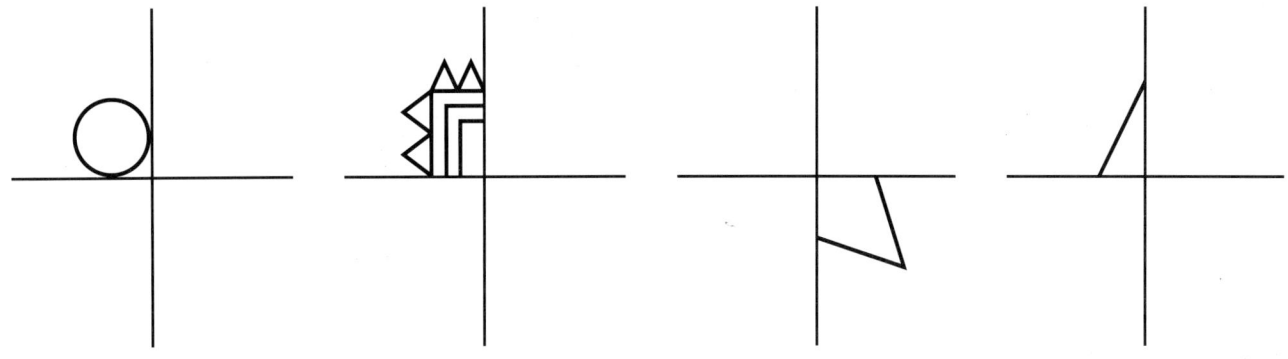

• •

Colour those which show rotational symmetry

Name: _____ Date: _____

AT3 Level 4

B Rotational symmetry C90

These shapes show rotational symmetry
Complete the pictures

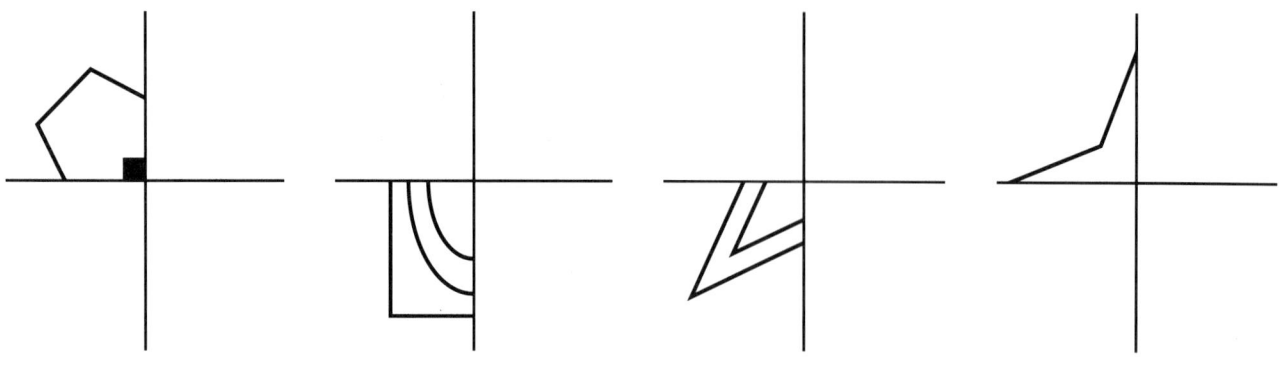

Colour those which show rotational symmetry

Name: _____ Date: _____

AT3 Level 4

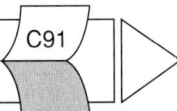

A | Measuring

Record these measurements, choosing appropriate tools and units

The circumference of a friend's forearm 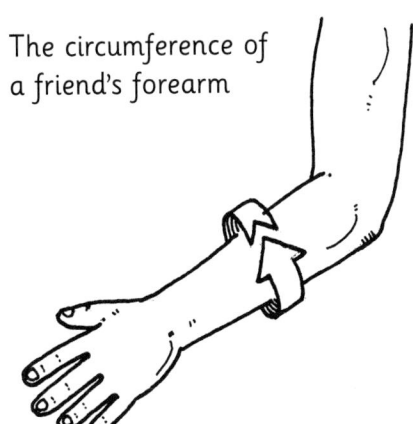 circumference =	The 'weight' of a PE bag  result =	The 'weight' of a parcel  result =
The dimensions of a doorway 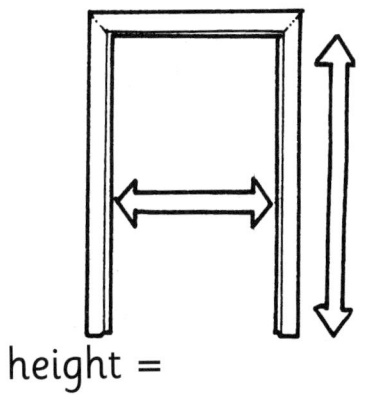 height = width =	The dimensions of a cardboard box 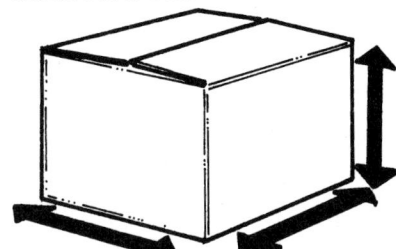 height = breadth = depth =	The length of the side of a die  length =
Capacity of a teapot  capacity =	Time taken to write down six important telephone numbers that you know time taken =	Time taken to skip round the playground with a skipping-rope time taken =

Name: _____ Date: _____

AT3 Level 4

| B | Measuring | C92 |

Record these measurements, choosing appropriate tools and units

The circumference of a football **or** a netball 	The dimensions of a table	The length of your foot 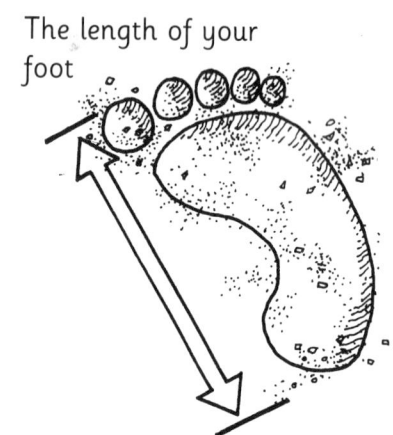
circumference =	length = breadth =	length =
Time taken for the class to line up	Capacity of a large bowl 	The dimensions of a book 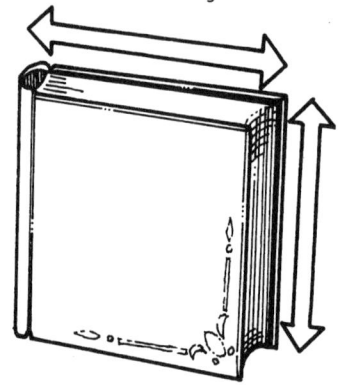
time taken =	capacity =	length = breadth =
'Weight' of a teacher 	'Weight' of an apple 	Time taken to complete a maths task
result =	result =	time taken =

A Perimeter and area

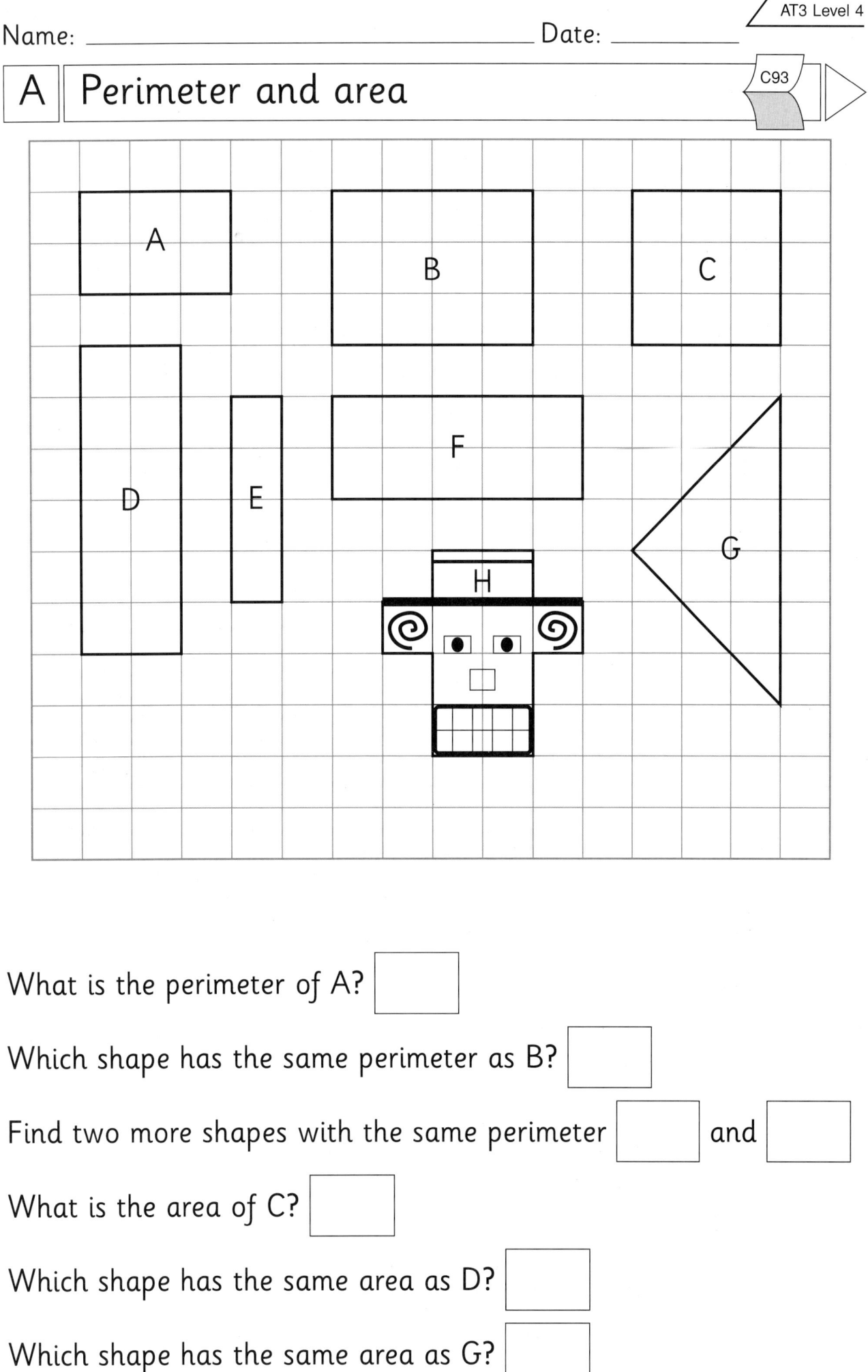

What is the perimeter of A? ☐

Which shape has the same perimeter as B? ☐

Find two more shapes with the same perimeter ☐ and ☐

What is the area of C? ☐

Which shape has the same area as D? ☐

Which shape has the same area as G? ☐

Name: _____ Date: _____

B | Perimeter and area

AT3 Level 4
C94

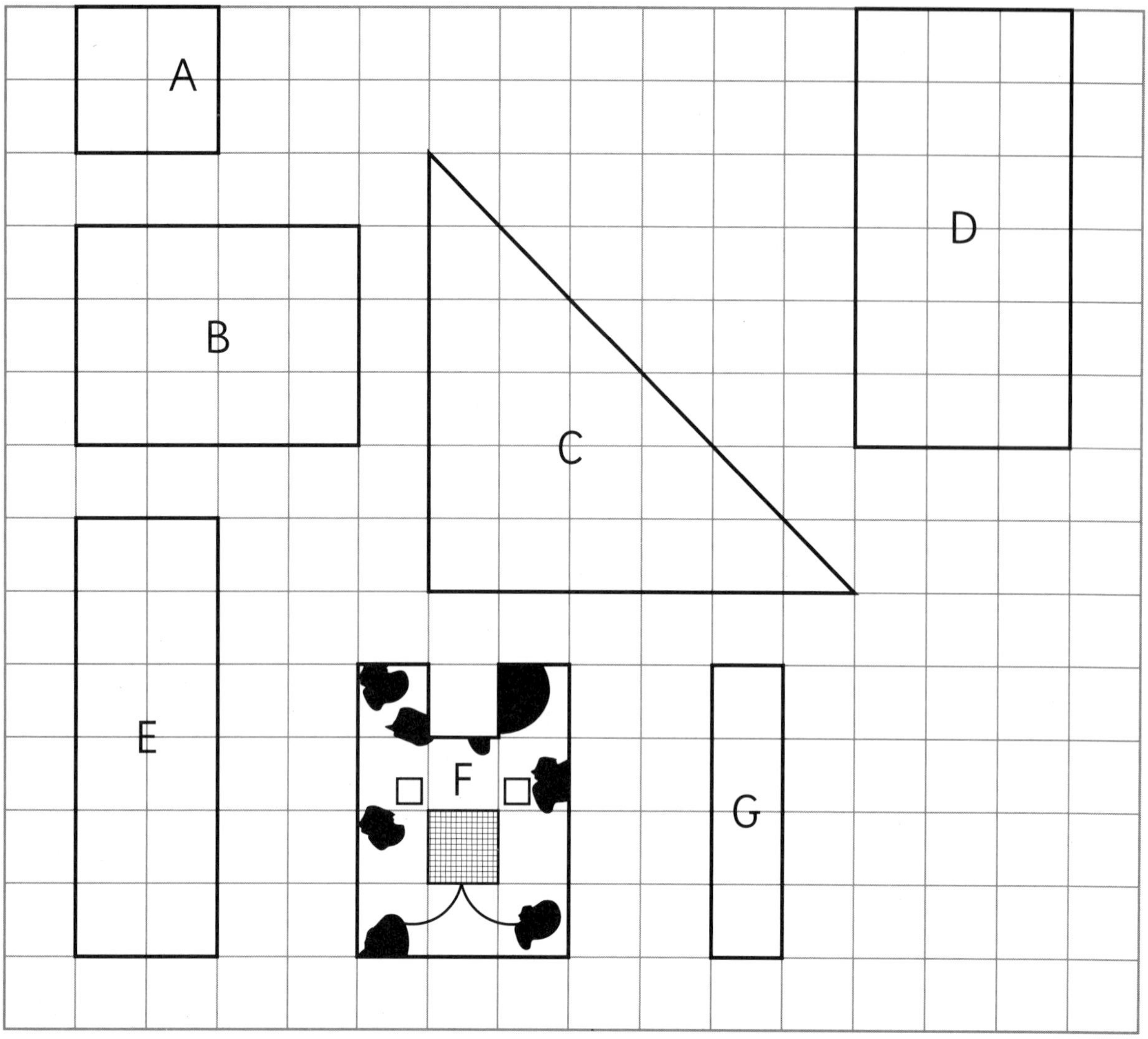

What is the perimeter of A? ☐

Which shape has the same perimeter as B? ☐

Find a shape to match C in area ☐

What is the area of F? ☐

Do A and G have the same perimeter or area? ☐

What is the area of E? ☐

A | Volume

AT3 Level 4

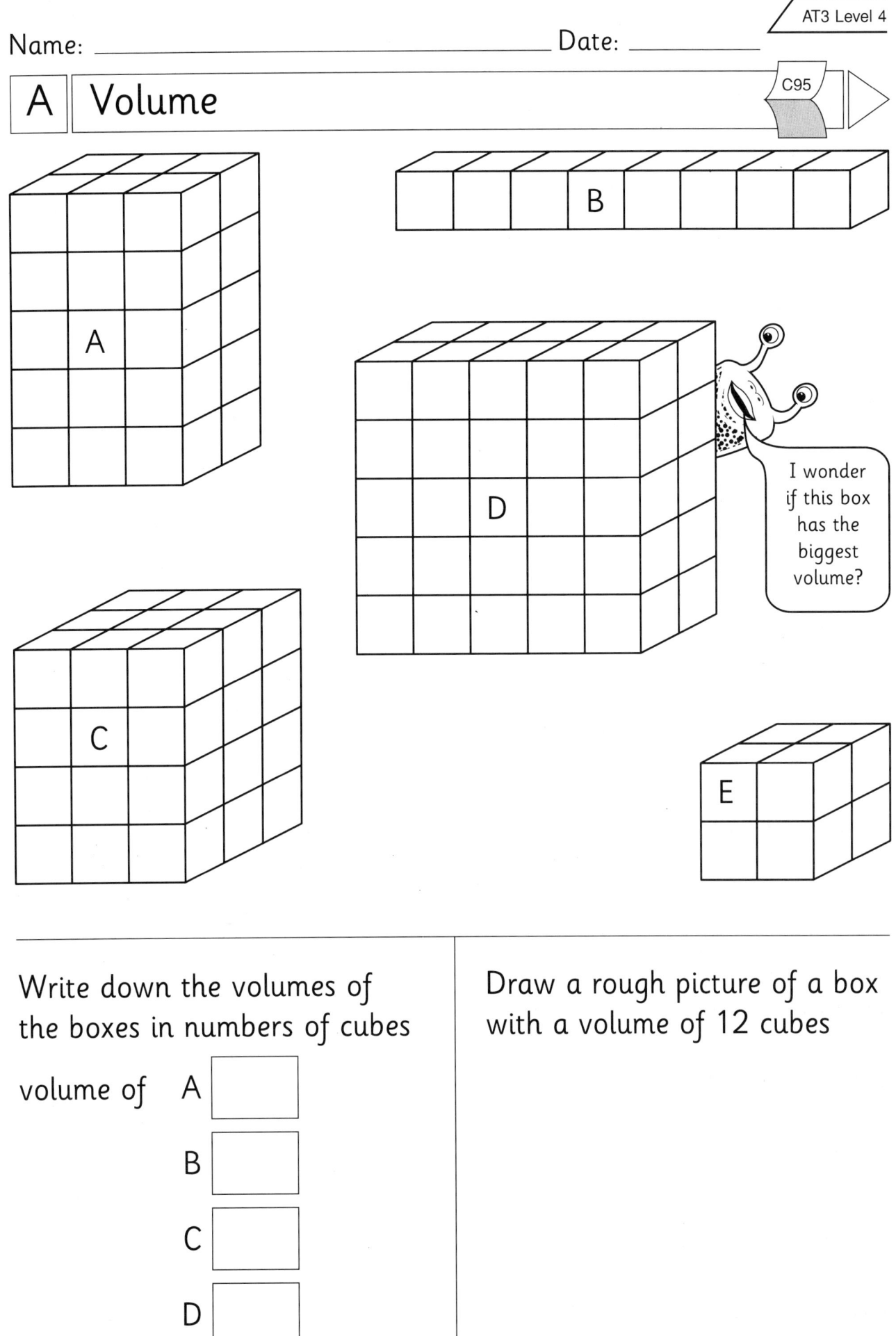

"I wonder if this box has the biggest volume?"

Write down the volumes of the boxes in numbers of cubes

volume of A ☐

B ☐

C ☐

D ☐

E ☐

Draw a rough picture of a box with a volume of 12 cubes

Name: _____ Date: _____

B | Volume

AT3 Level 4
C96

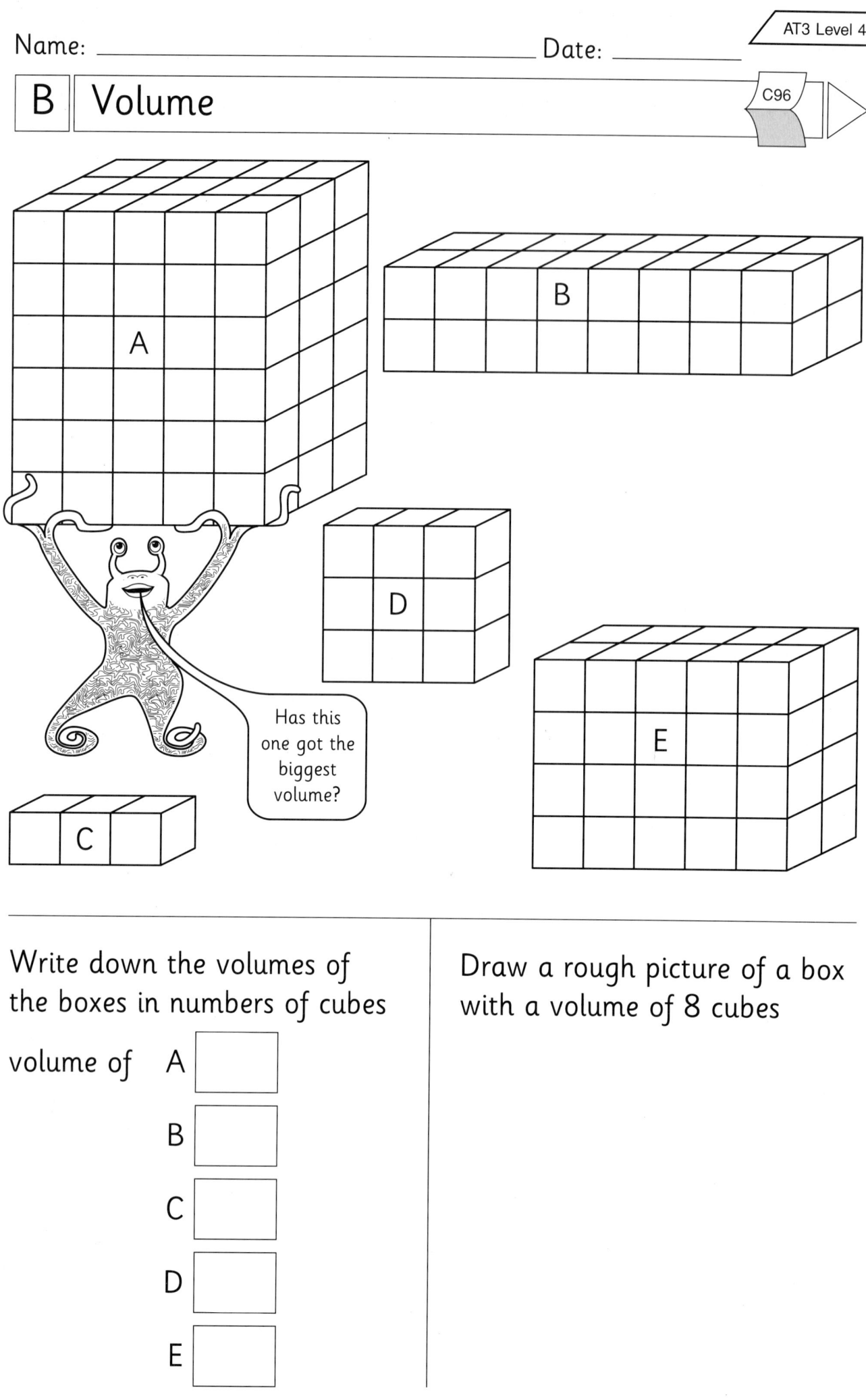

Has this one got the biggest volume?

Write down the volumes of the boxes in numbers of cubes

volume of A ☐
B ☐
C ☐
D ☐
E ☐

Draw a rough picture of a box with a volume of 8 cubes

Name: _____ Date: _____

AT3 Level 5

A | Accurate construction of 3-D models

C97

TEACHER'S RECORD

Can construct the following:

cube .... ❏

tetrahedron .... ❏

triangular prism .... ❏

hexagonal prism .... ❏

pyramid .... ❏

Remarks

Comments on accuracy of angles and 'fit' of sides in making a regular shape

Name: _____ Date: _____

AT3 Level 5

| B | Accurate construction of 3-D models | C98 |

Child's record

I have worked on these models	My evaluation of my work
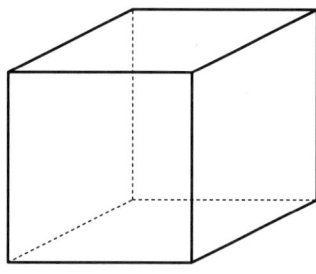 cuboid (or a cube)	
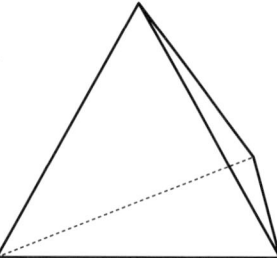 tetrahedron	
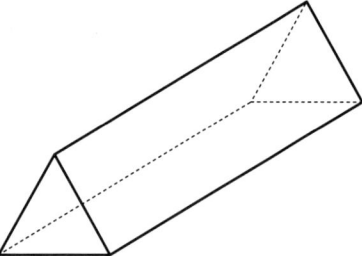 triangular prism	
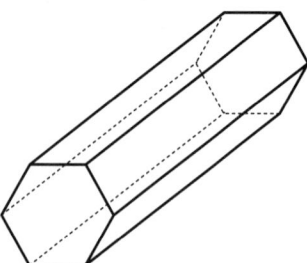 hexagonal prism	
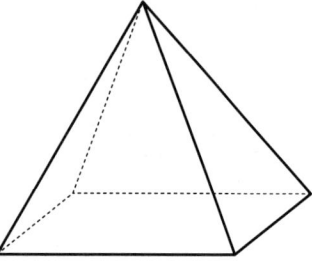 pyramid	

Name: _____ Date: _____

AT3 Level 5

A Angle language

C99

Look carefully at the lines and shapes below
Write in beside each one the word or words that describes it

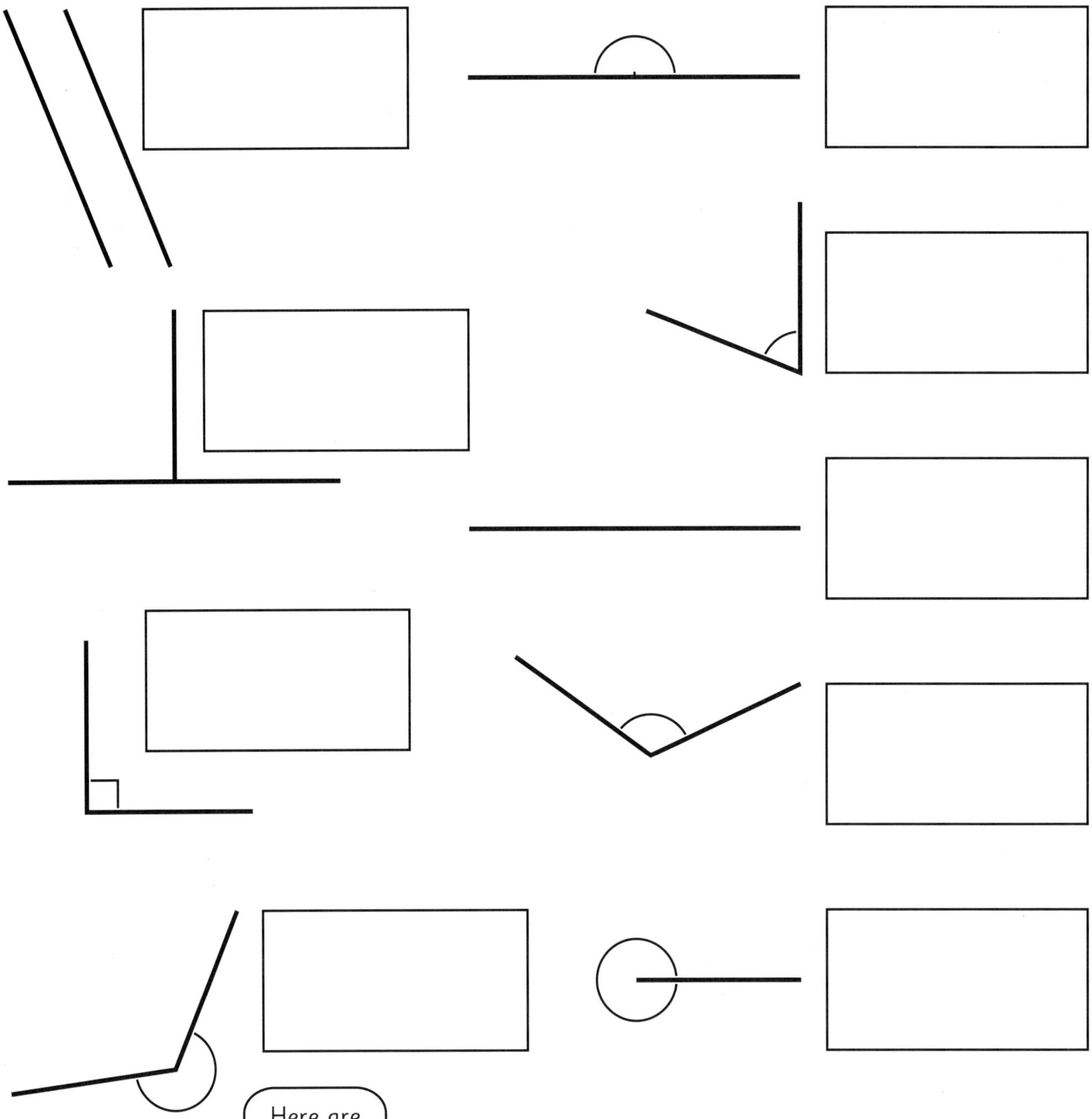

Here are the words to help you

- perpendicular
- acute angle
- straight angle
- revolution
- right angle
- obtuse angle
- reflex angle
- parallel lines
- horizontal

Name: _____ Date: _____

B | Angle language

AT3 Level 5

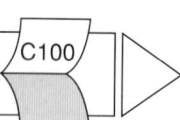

Join up the shapes and lines on the left of the page to the words that describe them

obtuse angle

revolution

parallel lines

reflex angle

perpendicular

straight angle

acute angle

right angle

horizontal

Name: _____ Date: _____

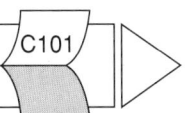

| A | Shape properties |

•angles •symmetry •other facts

Write here

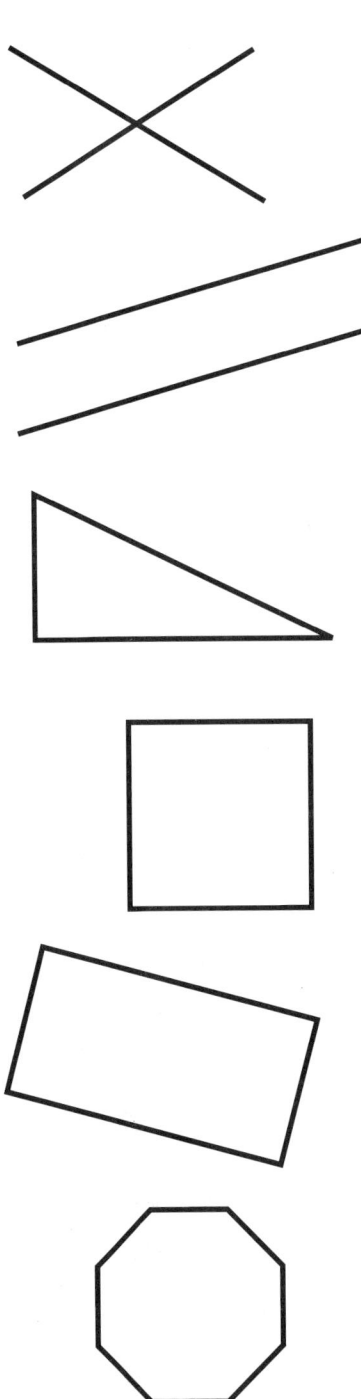

Name: _____ Date: _____

B | **Shape properties**

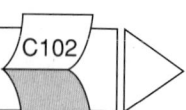

Write about these shapes – try angles, symmetry and other facts

•angles •symmetry •other facts

Write here

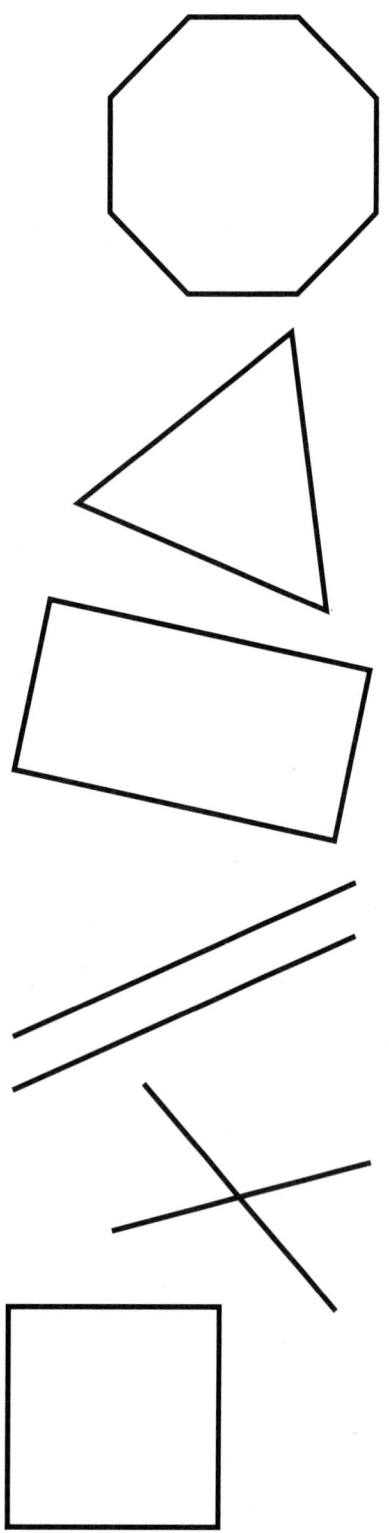

Name: _____ Date: _____

AT3 Level 5

A | Imperial/metric – measures/estimation

C103

Write down what these 'weigh', hold or measure in both kinds of units

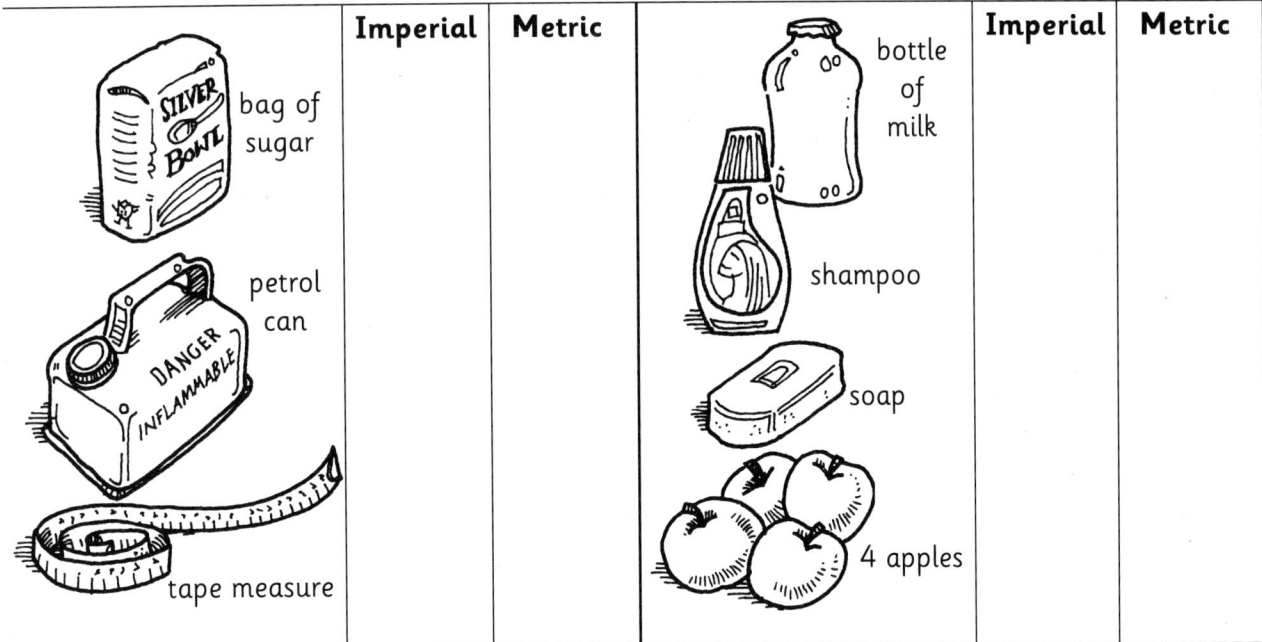

	Imperial	Metric		Imperial	Metric
bag of sugar			bottle of milk		
petrol can			shampoo		
tape measure			soap		
			4 apples		

Write in your estimates for these
Make them as accurate as you can

'weight' of a pair of PE pumps	
'weight' of a form or bench	
capacity of a mop bucket	
length of school front fence	
time taken to sharpen a pencil	
height of school caretaker	
time taken to change into games equipment and assemble ready to play rounders	

Name: _____ Date: _____

AT3 Level 5

B Imperial/metric – measures/estimation

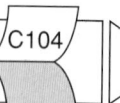
C104

Write down what these 'weigh', hold or measure in both kinds of units

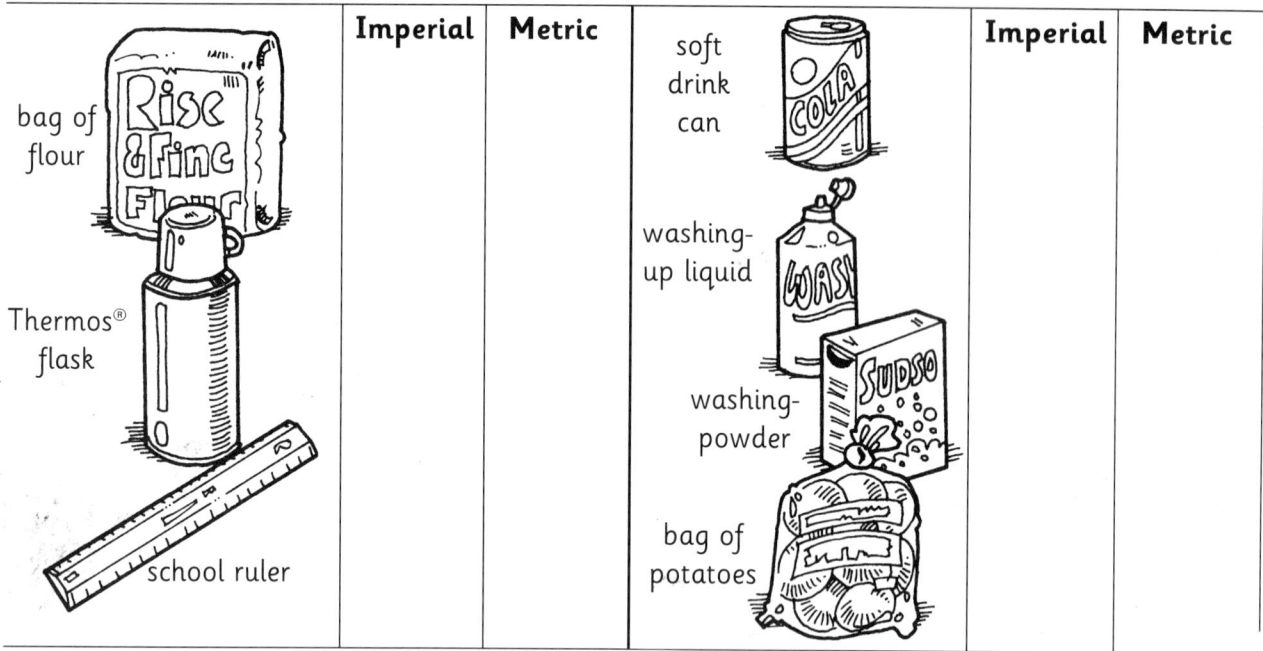

	Imperial	Metric		Imperial	Metric
bag of flour			soft drink can		
Thermos® flask			washing-up liquid		
school ruler			washing-powder		
			bag of potatoes		

Write in your estimates for these
Make them as accurate as you can

'weight' of a lunch box	
capacity of a fire bucket	
'weight' of a football	
length of a piano	
time taken to clean your classroom windows	
length of school entrance hall	
time taken to say your name and address	

Name: _____ Date: _____

AT4 Level 2

C105

A | Sorting objects

TEACHER'S RECORD

Sort a collection of items found in a cleaning cupboard .... ❑

Make subsets .... ❑

Draw results of sort .... ❑

••

Sort 2-D shape .... ❑

Make subsets .... ❑

Draw results of sorts .... ❑

••

Remarks

Name: _____ Date: _____

AT4 Level 2

| B | Sorting objects

C106

TEACHER'S RECORD

Sort a collection of items found in a desk ....❏

Make subsets ....❏

Draw results of sorts ....❏

•••

Sort 3-D shapes ....❏

Make subsets ....❏

Draw results of sorts ....❏

•••

Remarks

Name: _____ Date: _____

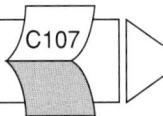

| A | Gather information/construct a table |

Indoor play

- Write down how many days there is indoor play in the morning
- Do this for 3 weeks – 15 days
- Put the information in a table

....

TV

- Name 3 TV programmes for children
- Ask 10 people which of these they watch
- Draw a block graph to show the results

This programme's good. What's it called?

I don't know but I always watch it!

Name: _____ Date: _____

B | Gather information/construct a table

AT4 Level 2

Things in the home
- Ask 10 people which of these they have at home
- Put the results in a block graph

Presents
- Ask 10 people which 3 things they would like for their birthday or Christmas
- Put the results in a table. Remember you could put things in groups. (For example roller boots and a football could be 'outdoor games' and computer games could all be called 'computer')

  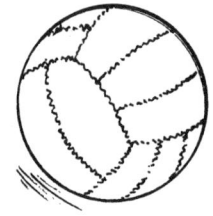

Name: _____ Date: _____

AT4 Level 3

C109

A Table/list

Hair and eyes
Here is a list showing the hair colour and eye colour of ten children

Angus	black/brown	**Belinda**	auburn/green
Gwen	brown/green	**Sue**	blond/green
Cynthia	brown/hazel	**April**	auburn/blue
Leo	blond/blue	**Yasmin**	black/hazel
Paul	blond/grey	**Ashra**	black/brown

How many children have black hair? ☐

Who are the hazel-eyed people? _____

Sue is blond. Who else is blond? _____

How many green-eyed people have brown hair? ☐

The local petshop stocks these items for cats and dogs

	cat	dog
collar	£1·85	£3·50
lead	—	£4.50
tinned food	41p	45p
dry crunch	£1·60 kg	£1·99 kg
vitamins	£2·35/100	£2·55/100
treats	55p	55p
toy	89p	£1.10

Which is the most expensive item? _____

How much would 100 vitamin tablets cost?

for a cat ☐   for a dog ☐

What things are cheaper than a cat toy?

_____

Name: _____ Date: _____

AT4 Level 3

| B | Table/list

C110

Lek is going to camp and needs to shop for things to put in a washbag

Shopping list

shampoo	95p
soap	35p
toothbrush	70p
toothpaste	75p
flannel	99p
nailbrush	67p
comb	50p

How much does Lek spend altogether? _____

Which things are cheaper than a nailbrush? _____

What could Lek buy for the same price as two bars of soap? _____

Destination	Departure time	Platform
Cardiff	7·02	7
Liverpool	7·36	15
Manchester	8·15	12
Bristol	8·31	3
Carlisle	8·45	1
Crewe	8·52	20

Which train leaves from platform 1? _____

Which trains leave before the Bristol train? _____
_____

Which train departs after 8.45? _____

Name: _____ Date: _____

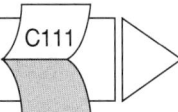

AT4 Level 3

A — Bar chart/pictogram construction

Toss a 2p and a 10p coin together 30 times
Put your results on a bar chart — remember to record when you get two heads, two tails, 2p head and 10p tail, and 10p head and 2p tail

Number of throws

2h/2t, h/t or t/h

• •

Find out how many children in each class belong to Brownies, Guides or Cub Scouts

Make a chart to show how many, drawing one 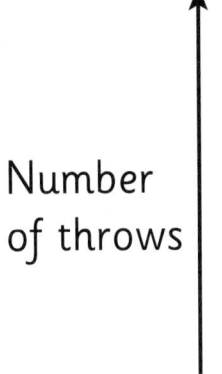 neckerchief for every five children

Number of

Brownies   Guides   Cub Scouts

Classes

Name: _____ Date: _____

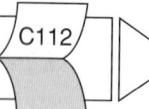

| B | Bar chart/pictogram construction |

Shuffle four different Happy Families or Snap cards

Turn up the top card
Do this 30 times
Write down which card is turned up
Put your results on a bar chart

Number of times cards are shuffled and turned over

Top card

....

Find out in which months the other children in the school have their birthdays and record what they say

Make a chart, drawing 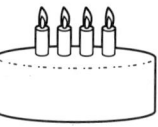 for each 10 children

Number of children

Month

Name: _____ Date: _____

AT4 Level 3

A | **Bar chart/pictogram interpretation**

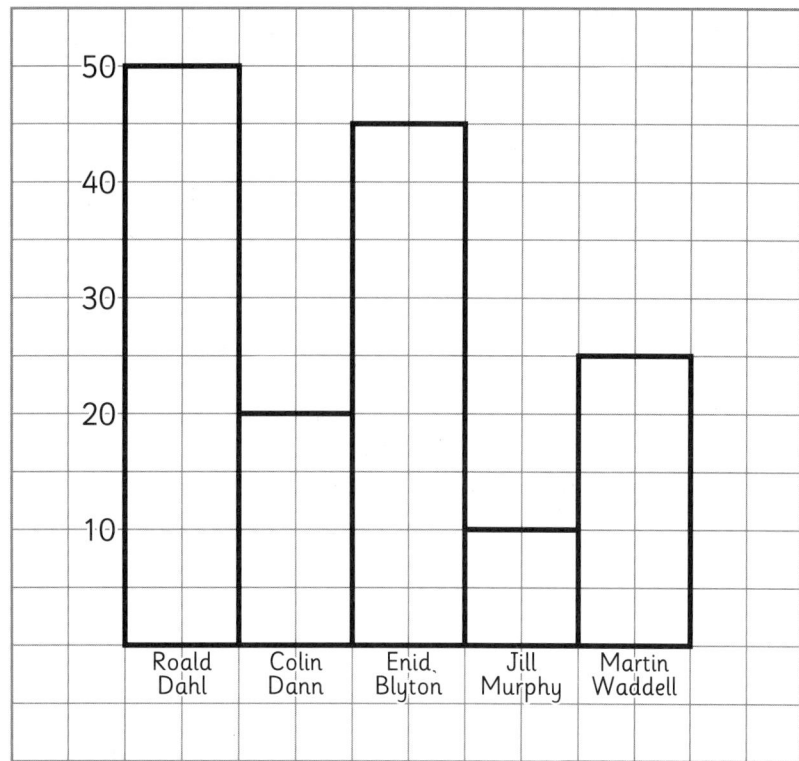

Who is the most popular author? _____

How many children voted for Colin Dann? ☐

Which author got 25 votes? _____

• •

Number of ice-creams sold by Ms Creemy

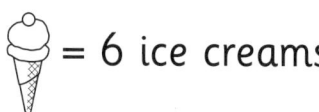 = 6 ice creams

Nut Surprise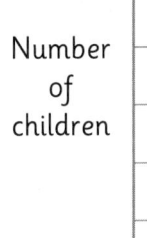

Pineapple Scrummy

Choc Double Oh

Strawberry Supremo

Which ice-cream was most popular? _____

How many Strawberry Supremos sold? ☐

Which ice-cream sold to 24 people? _____

Name: _____ Date: _____

AT4 Level 3

| B | Bar chart/pictogram interpretation |

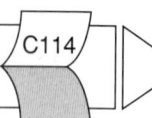

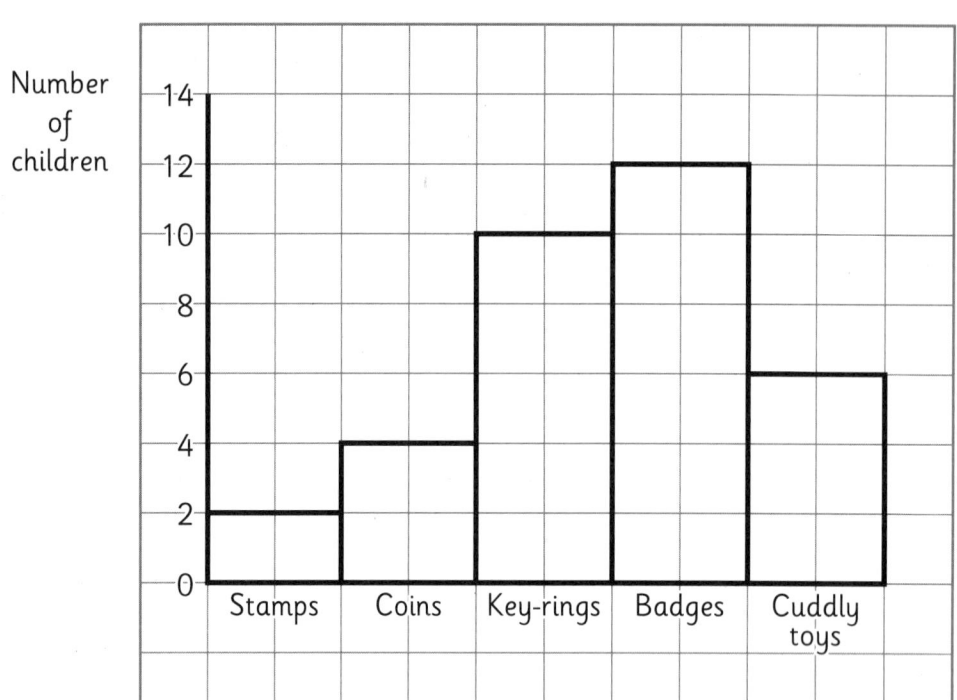

☐ people collect key-rings

Collecting _____ is the most popular

Four people collect _____

....

Results of a phone-in vote on the television for best behaved pet

= One hundred votes

Percy the kitten

Broom the dog

Hello the hamster

Rudolf the rabbit

Which pet was voted best behaved? _____

How many people voted for Rudolf? ☐

Which pet got 300 votes? _____

Name: _____ Date: _____   AT4 Level 4

A Interpret/construct frequency diagrams   C115

Sunny days The weather record for four weeks shows these sunny days

M	Monday	✻
T	Tuesday	✻ ✻ ✻
W	Wednesday	✻
Th	Thursday	✻ ✻
F	Friday	✻ ✻ ✻ ✻

How many sunny days are there altogether? ☐

Which day is sunniest?
(**M**, **T**, **W**, **Th** or **F**?) ☐

How many sunny Tuesdays were there? ☐

···

School dinner The menu reveals that these items are available over a six-week period.

week 1

week 2

week 3

week 4

week 5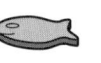

week 6

Which item is available in fewest weeks?

_____

In which week is there the biggest range of food?

_____

Which food is always available? _____

 – pizza   – toad-in-the-hole    – hot dog    – pasty

 – fish finger    – salad   – jacket potato

···

In discussion with your teacher, decide on what data to collect
Collect it and set it out in a frequency diagram
Attach your work to this sheet for marking

Name: _____ Date: _____ AT4 Level 4

B | Interpret/construct frequency diagrams C116

Rainy days The weather record for four weeks shows these rainy days

M Monday

T Tuesday

W Wednesday

Th Thursday

F Friday

How many rainy days are there altogether? ☐

Which day is wettest?
(**M**, **T**, **W**, **Th** or **F**?) ☐

On which day did it not rain? ☐

· ·

Use of quiet area Frequency table showing how many children used a classroom quiet area in one day, and what they did there

Reading   X X X X X X X X

Discussion   X X X X X

Thinking   X X

Recovering from
illness/accident   X

Sent there
– too noisy   X X X

Finishing
written work   X X X X X

Missing play   X X X

How many children used the quiet area? ☐

What did they do mostly?
_____

What is the quiet area least used for?
_____

How many children used the area for thinking or discussion? ☐

· ·

In discussion with your teacher decide on what data to collect
Collect it and set it out in a frequency diagram
Attach your work to this sheet for marking

Name: _____ Date: _____

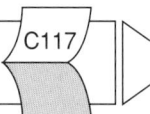

A | Frequency diagrams – median/mode

Tibby A cat was observed every 5 minutes for 3 hours
This is what Tibby was doing

Activity	Tally
looking through window	IIIIIII
asleep	IIIIIIIIIIIII
playing	III
washing/grooming	IIIIIIII
eating	IIII

Find out the frequency of each activity
Draw a graph showing Tibby's activities over the 3-hour research period

••

Cat show At a cat show a number of champions had their whiskers measured
The longest whisker measurements were these

	cm
Blackie	8·6
Simba	10·2
Angus	5·4
Custard	11·1
Marge	9·7
Whopper	9·5
Pinky	9·7
Sam	8·8
Dolly	9·9
Beauty	9·7

	cm
Em	7·3
Puss	7·9
Tinker	8·2
Shem	10·1
Socks	9·7
Blackie	9·7
Big ears	9·4
Tiger	8·7
Moggy	7·6
Felix	7·8

Find the following:

Median whisker length [ ]   Mode whisker length [ ]

Draw a bar-line graph showing whisker length

Who deserves the Whisker Champion rosette? _____

Name: _____ Date: _____

AT4 Level 4

| B | Frequency diagrams – median/mode

C118

Savoury biscuits

This list shows the number of savoury biscuits in a variety of small packs

cheesy triangles	36
cheesy circles	42
cheesy squares	35
cheesy rectangles	27

savoury sticks	35
savoury snacks	37
savoury chunks	36
savoury knots	35

mini shapes	29
mini crunch	31
mini chews	32
mini bites	35

Find the median number of biscuits ☐

Find the mode ☐

Draw a block graph to show how many biscuits there were in each pack

···

Cooking biscuits

Here are the oven temperatures and cooking times for a variety of biscuits

	temperature (°C)	time (minutes)
oatcakes	180	25
shortbread	160	45
savoury twists	220	12
cheese fingers	200	10
petit fours	190	20
crumbles	150	25
cheese straws	230	7

Draw a graph comparing oven temperature and cooking time
What are your conclusions about the relationship between oven temperature and cooking time?

Name: _____ Date: _____

AT4 Level 4

C119

A | 'Likelihood', 'evens' and 'fair'

List of 'likelihood' events to discuss
- I will fall over today
- I will oversleep tomorrow morning and be late for school
- My family will win a competition next week
- There will be ice-cream for pudding tonight
- I will finish my reading book today
- It will snow on Saturday

Understands 'likelihood' and 'chance' ☐

....

'Evens' situation

If the Happy Families cards Mr Fuse, Mrs Fuse, Fanny Fuse and Freddy Fuse, the electrician's family, are put face down on the table, what is the chance of turning up Freddy Fuse?

If Donny Drip the plumber's son was added to these, what is the chance of turning up Fanny Fuse?

☐

....

'Fair'/'unfair'

Two players have their own dice for a game
One dice has 1 – 6 on it, the other is 12 sided (1 – 12)

Who wins?

Is it fair?

Can say why not 'fair' ☐

....

Name: _____ Date: _____

AT4 Level 4

B 'Likelihood', 'evens' and 'fair'

C120

List of 'likelihood' events to discuss
- I shall get a knot in my trainer lace at the weekend
- I will see an elephant tomorrow
- I will finish all the schoolwork given me today
- My cousin will invite me to a picnic soon
- I shall go to the cinema next week
- My family will get a parcel in the post tomorrow

Understands 'likelihood' and 'chance' ☐

'Evens' situation

If you are offered a green sweet and an orange sweet, each hidden in a hand, what is the likelihood of you choosing the hand with the orange sweet in it?

If there are three sweets hidden; green, orange and red, what are the chances of choosing the red one?

Can say why not 'evens' ☐

'Fair'/'unfair'

In a sweet mixture there are twice as many round sweets as oval ones. If they are shared so that Kim has round ones and Jim has oval ones, is this fair?

Can say why not 'fair'/'unfair' ☐

Name: _____ Date: _____

AT4 Level 5
C121

A Mean and range

Mum and Dad want Shirley to stop using the phone so much. Mum said that an average phone call only takes 3 or 4 minutes.

Shirley's calls (minutes and seconds) 4:20, 7:13, 5:57, 5:04, 8:57, 15:26, 18:03, 12:11, 14:11, 3:05, 4:45, 6:03, 3:03, 5:34, 5:06

What is the average length of call that Shirley makes? ☐

What is the range of lengths of times for Shirley's calls? ☐

• •

Bumbles Haulage is a transport company based in London.

(Distance from London in miles)
Birmingham 105, Brighton 52, Bristol 122, Edinburgh 378, Exeter 172, Leeds 189, Liverpool 202, Nottingham 122, Oxford 57, Sheffield 159, York, 193

What is the mean distance travelled by their lorries in visiting these cities? ☐

What range of distances can they boast that their lorries travel? ☐

Name: _____ Date: _____

AT4 Level 5

B Mean and range

Big supermarkets often buy fruit and vegetables that are fairly uniform in size.

Here are the 'weights' of some apples of the same variety
140 g, 137 g, 129 g, 135·5 g, 141·2 g, 142 g, 145 g, 143·4 g, 139 g, 137·2 g, 140·8 g, 145·6 g, 139 g, 142 g, 140 g, 142 g, 136·9 g, 140 g, 137 g, 140 g

What is the mean 'weight'? ☐

What is the range of 'weights'? ☐

• •

Here are sunshine figures for a number of towns in Devon and Cornwall

Name of town	Average number of hours of sunshine per day (July/August)
Barnstaple	7·6
Ilfracombe	9·3
Tavistock	8·4
Plymouth	6·2
Brixham	7·8
Newton Abbot	8·1
Tiverton	8·2
Penzance	7·5
St Ives	10·0
Helston	8·5

What is the mean number of hours of sunshine? ☐

What is the range of hours of sunshine? ☐

Name: _____ Date: _____

AT4 Level 5

| A | Construct/interpret statistical diagrams

Of the children's books sold in a leading book shop these are the proportions sold of each subject stocked by the shop.

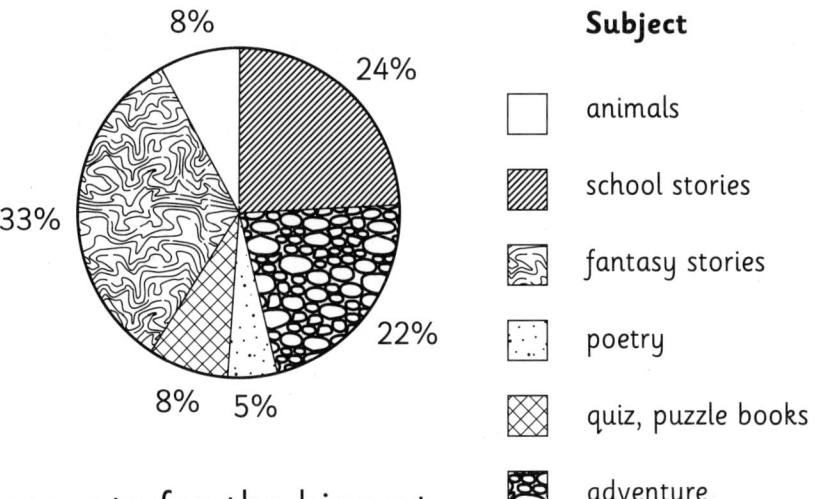

Subject
- animals
- school stories
- fantasy stories
- poetry
- quiz, puzzle books
- adventure

What kind of book accounts for the biggest proportion of sales? _____

What percentage of books sold are poetry books? ☐

What sort of books account for 22% of sales?
_____

••

In a class of children in a village school there are twelve 7-year-olds, six 8-year-olds and two 6-year-olds. Draw a pie chart to show the composition of the class

••

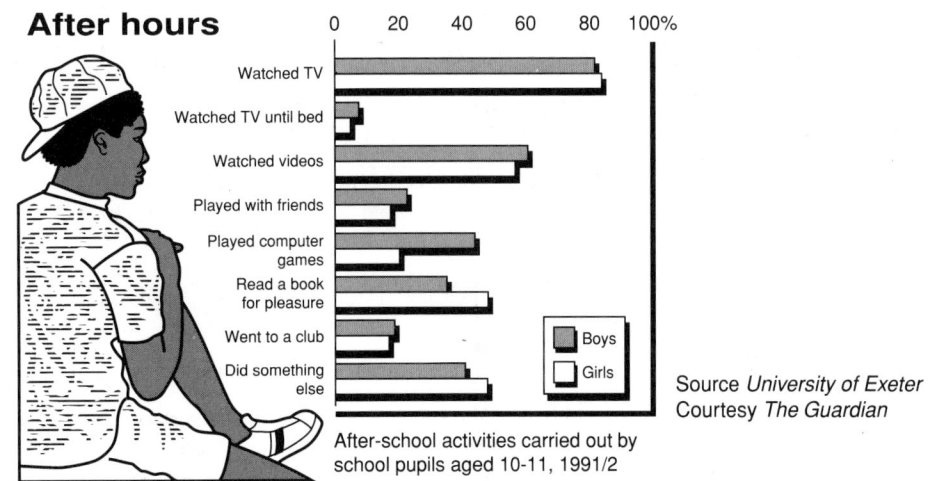

From the above chart, write a short report on what 10-year-olds and 11-year-olds do after school. Point out what they do most, what they do least, and the similarities and differences between boys and girls.

Name: _____ Date: _____

AT4 Level 5

B Construct/interpret statistical diagrams C124

A children's TV programme ran an art competition. The pie chart shows the percentage of entries done in a variety of media.

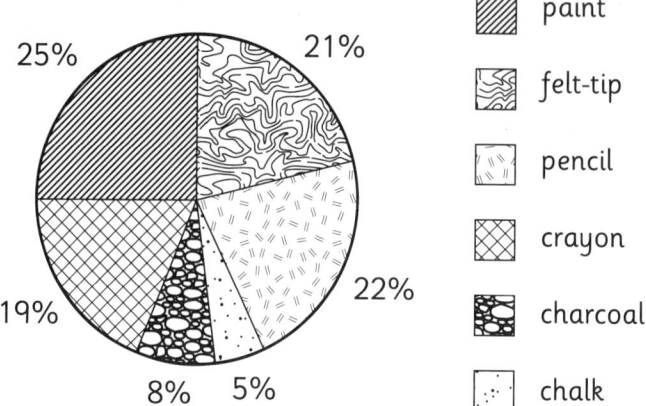

What percentage of entries were done in charcoal? ☐

What does the '25%' show? _____

What percentage of entries were either crayon or pencil? ☐

• •

In a primary school, records showed that 40 children had no brothers or sisters, 72 children had at least one sister, 48 children had at least one brother and 20 children had at least one brother and one sister. Draw a pie chart to show these figures as percentages.

• •

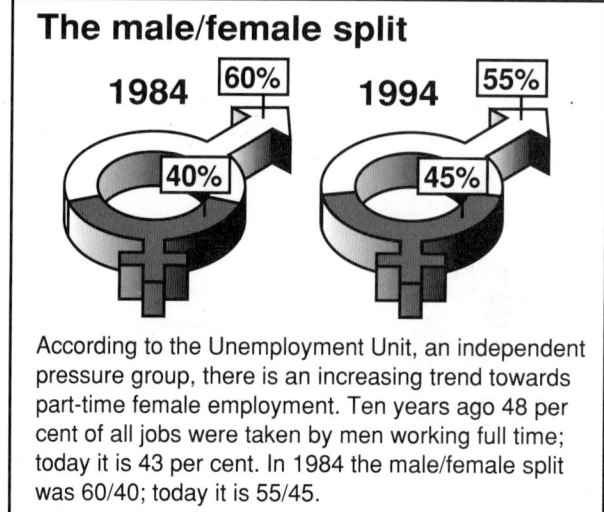

According to the Unemployment Unit, an independent pressure group, there is an increasing trend towards part-time female employment. Ten years ago 48 per cent of all jobs were taken by men working full time; today it is 43 per cent. In 1984 the male/female split was 60/40; today it is 55/45.

Courtesy *The Guardian*

Write a report on changes in the percentages of men and women in jobs, using the data above to help you.

A | Estimate and justify probabilities

AT4 Level 5
C125

1

Here is a variety of school meals.
How likely is it that these will be on offer at your school tomorrow?

If your school does not provide meals, or you never have had a school dinner, make predictions based on what you know about school meals.
Draw and name each meal at some point along the 'likelihood' line above.
Justify your decisions.

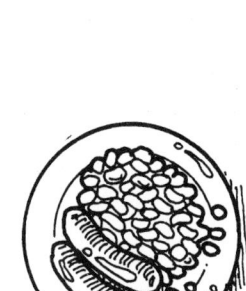
vegetable pasty
cabbage
mashed potato

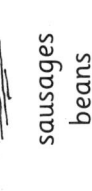
hot dog

pizza
mashed potato
salad

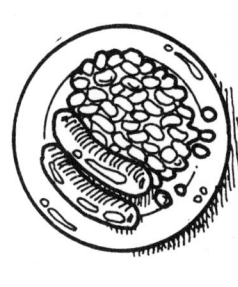
sausages
beans

chicken
chips
peas

B | Estimate and justify probabilities | C126

1

1 —

0 —

At sunset the sky sometimes appears to be a variety of colours.

Write each of these colours on the line above to show how likely you think it is to appear in the sky at sunset tomorrow. Justify your decisions.

Red Yellow Blue
Orange Green Violet
Pink White Grey

AT4 Level 5

AT4 Level 5

Name: _____ Date: _____

A Listing all possible outcomes C127

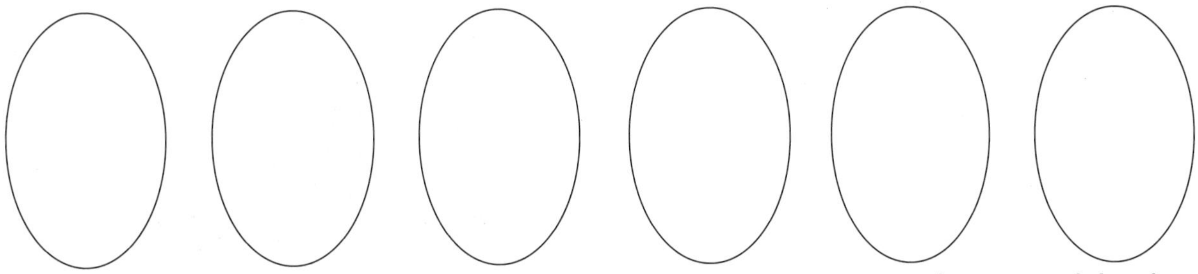

red   blue   yellow   green   pink   black

Poppy   Google   Zimmy   Twiz   Ced   Smiler

A monster egg manufacturer puts a monster gift inside each egg
The eggs come wrapped in one of six colours

List all the possible outcomes in terms of gift and wrapper colour

Name: _____ Date: _____

B | Listing all possible outcomes

AT4 Level 5
C128

A class of children are asked to line up in two lines or columns

line 1   line 2

As each pair comes through the classroom door, think about the possible arrangements of girls and boys
Draw up a table to show what might happen

Record Sheet 1 Class Record

Class	Level		Date		
			Teacher's name		
Name		AT1	AT2	AT3	AT4

Record Sheet 2 Child's Record

Name	Date of birth	Teacher's Initials

Level 2

AT1	Date	AT2	Date	AT3	Date	AT4	Date
1 Select/talk maths		1 Add/sub to 10/nos to 100		1 2-D/3-D names		1 Sort objects	
2 Maths lang/diag		2 Halves/quarters		2 Movement		2 Gather info/construct table	
3 What if?		3 Number patterns		3 Right angles			
				4 Length/mass			

Level 3

AT1	Date	AT2	Date	AT3	Date	AT4	Date
4 Solve problems		4 Big numbers		5 Sort shapes		3 Table/list	
5 Organize, check		5 Decimal money/approx		6 Reflective symmetry		4 Bar chart construct	
6 General statement		6 Negative numbers		7 Length/capacity/mass/time		5 Bar chart interpret	
		7 Add/subtract to 20					
		8 2, 5, 10 x tables					
		9 Multiply/divide					
		10 Remainders					
		11 Patterns/computations					

Level 4

AT1	Date	AT2	Date	AT3	Date	AT4	Date
7 Problem solving		12 Place value		8 Construct 2-D/3-D		6 Frequency diags	
8 Present info		13 Computation		9 Congruence		7 Median/mode	
9 Pattern search		14 Calculator		10 Rotational symmetry		8 'Likelihood'	
		15 Fractions/percent		11 Measuring			
		16 Patterns/multiples		12 Perimeter/area			
		17 Formulae/words		13 Volume			
		18 Coords in 1st quadrant					

Level 5

AT1	Date	AT2	Date	AT3	Date	AT4	Date
10 Carry through task		19 × ÷ 10, 100, 1,000		14 3-D models		9 Mean/range	
11 Use symbols		20 Neg nos/decimals		15 Angle language		10 Stat diagram	
12 Generalizations		21 Fractions/percent		16 Shape		11 Probabilities	
		22 Multiply/divide		17 Measure/estimate		12 All possible outcomes	
		23 Formulae					